A Field Guide to
Boys and Girls

A Field Guide to
Boys AND Girls

Differences, Similarities:
Cutting-Edge Information Every
Parent Needs to Know

SUSAN GILBERT

HarperCollins*Publishers*

HarperCollins books may be purchased for educational, business, or sales promotional use. For information please write: Special Markets Department, HarperCollins Publishers, Inc., 10 East 53rd Street, New York, NY 10022.

FIRST EDITION

Designed by Nancy B. Field

Library of Congress Cataloging-in-Publication Data

Gilbert, Susan, 1956–
    A field guide to boys and girls: differences, similarities: cutting-edge information every parent needs to know/Susan Gilbert.—1st ed.
      p. cm.
   ISBN 0-06-019371-9
    1. Child development   2. Child rearing.   3. Sex differences
(Psychology) in children. I. Title.
   HQ772.G465 2000
   305.231—dc21   00-027591

---

00 01 02 03 04 ❖/RRD 10 9 8 7 6 5 4 3 2 1

For my family

Contents

Foreword

Raising children has never been an easy job. Part of the difficulty in raising girls and boys results from the generation gap. Cultural beliefs change from one generation to the next, especially in the realm of sex roles. The cultural beliefs we grew up with are not the dominant beliefs as we raise our own children. For example, the answers to questions such as, "Should a girl be encouraged to do mathematics?" "Should a girl be discouraged from showing how smart she is?" "Should a boy be given a doll or a tea set?" change with the decades. Even parents' ideas of medical problems with respect to gender have changed with time. Girls projected to be very tall are no longer given hormones in an attempt to stop their growth, yet boys projected to be short are still sometimes given growth hormones.

Just as some questions change over time in child rearing, questions also change in science. Decades ago, when I began a career in developmental psychology, studying issues of gender was not "politically correct." Nevertheless, as more and more women entered academic research in the 1970s, they did study gender and it has now become a recognized subject of inquiry

But as gender research became acceptable, new questions arose. Historically, social scientists had studied males almost exclusively. Should only girls and women be studied in order to redress the bias created by this practice? Or should both females and males be studied to assess the validity of alleged differences, and to understand their causes? Some gender researchers did opt to study only girls and women; others opted to include males.

Some of the impetus for bringing gender into academic research was the feminist movement of the 1970s and 1980s. Those of us who studied females and males faced additional problems. By finding differences, would we betray our feminist ideals? Many of us believed, perhaps naively, that the first task was to learn all we could about gender. We believed, and I still believe, that pointing out the culture's beliefs and practices about gender would free both females and males. We particularly believed that understanding the causes of gender differences, biological and social, would allow people, especially parents, to make educated choices about their lives and the lives of their children.

And what have we learned after decades of studying gender? As scientists, we have learned a lot. But can the information from our myriad studies, approached in different ways, help parents? Scientists have not always been able to translate their findings into usable information for the general public.

This "field guide" provides a missing link. Susan Gilbert has carefully assembled information from decades of research and made it accessible to parents as they go about the task of raising girls and boys. She clearly summarizes the relevant findings while making sure to point out the limitations of the research. Her explanations and suggestions will help countless parents integrate scientific findings into the ongoing adventure of raising the best possible daughters and sons.

Carol Nagy Jacklin, Ph.D.

Carol Nagy Jacklin, a pioneer in gender research, is Professor Emeritus, Department of Psychology, University of Southern California. Her publications on gender include the germinal book (with Eleanor Maccoby) *The Psychology of Sex Differences* (1974), and the four-volume *The Psychology of Gender* (1992).

Acknowledgments

This book could not have been written without the many researchers, health care professionals, educators, and parents who set aside a lot of time for interviews. Thank you. In addition, several friends and colleagues were especially helpful in sharing personal stories and insights about boys and girls, as well as giving me a much-needed reality check on the scientific findings: Kim Loretucci, Joe Esposito, Rachel Sunshine, Marilyn Rottersman, Karen Prince, Laura Lilienfield, Susan Richman, Mary Reynolds, Robin Allen, Sarah Ball, Annesa Chan, Susan Marshall, Suzanne MacNeille, Kay Cahill, Linda Jo Platt, and Faye Chaplin. I am grateful to my agent, Kris Dahl, for her invaluable guidance, and to my editor, Trena Keating, for her sleight of hand with the manuscript. Finally, to my husband, Perry King, and our children, David and Sarah, I thank you for your love and encouragement, as well as for a wealth of raw material.

Introduction

Boys and Girls:
How Different?

About a dozen preschoolers are gathered at the library for the weekly story time. The girls are sitting on the floor, eyes riveted on the librarian, waiting for her to begin reading. But the librarian can't begin because most of the boys are chasing one another around the room, confounding their mothers' or nannies' efforts to get them to sit down. The expressions on the adults' faces suggest what they're thinking: "It figures. Boys will be boys, girls will be girls. The boys are wild, the girls are obedient. That's the way things are."

On another afternoon, things are different. Two of the girls from the library group are having a play date. They're out of control, tearing from room to room like the devilish Thing One and Thing Two in *The Cat in the Hat*. The host girl's mother tries to get them to sit quietly and draw, but they're too revved up. When the guest's mother comes for her daughter, the girl refuses to leave. The mother asks her daughter several times to put on her shoes, each time with a harder edge to her voice and each time to no avail. Finally, the mother picks up her daughter and her shoes and carries them out the door. The girl kicks, cries, and calls her mother names. So much for all that sugar and spice stuff—girls are as rambunctious and as defiant as boys.

Or are they? It's another afternoon, and the host girl has another friend over, this time one of the wild boys from the library. Only today he's not wild, and neither is she. First, they sit at a table and draw. Then they get on the floor and build together with blocks. Then they play a computer game. Maybe boys aren't so wild after all. Or maybe girls have a calming influence on boys. Or maybe. . . Oh, who knows?

But we want to know. Get a group of parents together, and one of the liveliest topics of conversation is bound to be the perceived differences between boys and girls: Who's easier? Who's better behaved? Who's better at what? Many of today's parents are surprised to find themselves asking these questions, especially those who came to parenting with the view that children are children and that looking for gender differences is looking for trouble because it can lead to gender bias. Still, we can't help but wonder just how different boys and girls really are. Everyone's got an opinion and an observation to back it up. So we look to scientists to sort out the confusion and explain boys and girls—our sons and daughters—to us.

Fortunately for parents, these are fertile times for research on gender differences in children. Neuroscientists using medical imaging technology can see that girls' and boys' brains look and operate somewhat differently. These differences are now thought to influence an array of characteristics in children: how fast they reach certain developmental milestones, how they play, the toys they like, and even some aspects of their personalities. Psychologists viewing slow-motion videos of mothers and infants can see that sons behave differently with their mothers than daughters do, even when their mothers treat them basically the same. But, of course, it should come as no surprise that researchers are also finding that parents, despite their best efforts, do treat their sons and daughters differently and that these differences, in turn, can contribute to disparities in boys' and girls' behavior, temperament, academic performance, and even health.

This book pulls together the latest research on the differences between boys and girls into a resource for parents. In addition to research, there are stories from dozens of parents, including gender researchers who are parents, with insights into their own daughters and sons, insights intended to help you better understand your children. The focus is on children from birth to age 12 because the gender issues that come to the fore during adolescence could fill several books themselves.

The chapters are organized into topics that often come up when parents talk about ways that gender seems to affect children. Chapter 1 begins literally at the beginning with pregnancy and the science of sex development, including sex differences in the brain, during fetal life until age 2. The chapter separates fact from fiction regarding common notions about baby girls and boys—whether it's possible for a pregnant woman to "tell" with any accuracy what she's having and whether sex is at all a factor in how easy or fussy, cooperative or defiant, an infant or a toddler is.

The other chapters follow the child as he or she grows. Chapter 2 looks at the extent to which gender influences a child's basic personality: How social a child is, how emotional, how fearful, how aggressive, and so on. Chapter 3 discusses gender-typed play and attitudes in children: Why it is that, even in the most gender-equitable homes, boys invariably reach a point when they act like boys in the traditional sense and girls act like girls. Many boys seem naturally drawn to trucks and often fairly rough play, for example, while many girls want to wear dresses even if their mothers live in jeans, and spend untold amounts of time tending to their dolls. The chapter will reassure you that if you see your child behaving like a stereotype, it's not because you failed but because your child is working hard to figure out what it means to be a boy or a girl. It's no coincidence that stereotypical behavior tends to kick into high gear once a child realizes his or her sex. The child is just trying to play the part.

Chapter 4 explores the real and perceived gender differences in academic performance and sports. It revisits and lays to rest lingering questions about whether girls and boys are naturally talented in certain subjects. For example, are boys better at math? Are girls better at writing? It looks at the strides that have been made to eliminate inequities that have long existed in the classroom, as well as in organized sports. Chapter 5 is devoted to the newest area of gender research: gender differences in health. Although boys and girls may be equally prone to common ailments like colds and flu, they have different risks for several other conditions, including asthma, attention deficit-hyperactivity disorder, depression, and even some forms of cancer. The chapter examines why these different risks exist and, more important, points to ways that you and your doctor can protect your children.

At the end of each chapter are suggestions on how you can use the research on gender development to benefit your sons and daughters. The focus is on ways that you can help your children be strong and confident; rise above the gender stereotypes; and avoid the social, academic, and health problems that hit boys or girls especially hard. The advice comes from leaders in the field of gender research, many of whom are parents. The suggestions they give are things that worked for them or that they'd do if they were raising children all over again.

Before you go any further, there are some things you should know. Above all, not everything you're about to read will apply to your children and other children you know. Gender research is about groups of boys and girls, not individuals. So, when research shows, for example, that girls talk earlier than boys and talk more thereafter, it means girls as a *group* compared with boys as a *group*. It doesn't mean that your daughter talked earlier or talks more than your son or than the boy next door. And if your child doesn't fit the group mold all the way down the line, that doesn't mean that he or she is abnormal. It simply underscores your child's individuality and drives home the point that even though scientists can categorize many aspects of our behavior and thought processes, there are still some things about each and every one of us that defy categorizing.

When it comes to gender-typed behavior, most children don't fit the mold. Even when researchers find differences between boys and girls, the differences are fairly minor, and it's often fewer than half the children who skew the results. For example, one of the biggest gender differences is that boys play rougher than girls, meaning that they're more likely to pummel, wrestle, and mock-fight each other. But even this difference isn't so great. It's a relatively small number of the boys—15 to 20 percent, according to one study—who score higher than *any* of the girls in assessments of rough-and-tumble play. So, most boys and girls fall within the same range. In this vast majority, some of the boys play rougher than some of the girls, some of the girls play rougher than some of the boys, and some of the boys and girls are equally rough.

What this means for those of us who are doing fieldwork everyday—that is, parents observing our children—is that we're bound to see more variation between any two children, regardless of their sex, than we'll see between a group of boys and a group of girls. One girl likes to play with Barbies; another likes to climb trees. One boy is energetic and athletic; another is lethargic. And children can change. The tree-climbing girl may suddenly want to bring Barbies into her tree house. The amount of variation we see depends on the mix of children, as well as on when and where we're watching them. Boys and girls look more alike when they're closely supervised by an adult—in class, for example—than when they're out at recess. At recess they have more freedom from adults but less freedom from the influence of classmates, who tend to encourage gender-typed play.

Aside from the individual-versus-group issue, there are other reasons why some of the findings on gender development may not ring true to you. Virtually all of them are based on a relatively small sliver of society: middle-class white children. The fact that many of the findings are seen in children in cultures around the world gives them some credibility, but it doesn't ensure that they apply to the diversity of girls and boys in the United States who are not middle class and white.

It's also important to understand the motivations of gender researchers. Gender research is political. There are scientists in the field of evolutionary psychology who stress biological differences and tend to play down the role that gender bias plays in shaping a child's behavior and achievement. For example, those scientists may look at the math SAT scores over the past 20 years, see that boys have consistently outperformed girls and conclude that it's because boys are naturally superior in math, not because teachers and parents have long discouraged girls from going beyond the minimum math requirement. Feminist researchers take the opposite view, pointing up the many ways that we treat boys and girls differently and how, in doing so, we make them more different than they really are.

With such hidden agendas, it's no wonder that gender research itself has been terribly biased over the years. To be sure, the first three-quarters of the twentieth century were full of pronouncements—all made in the name of science—on males' superior intelligence, athletic potential, and leadership qualities. But you don't have to go back that far to read arguments filled with "scientific" evidence that gender stereotypes are true. Consider this passage from *Brain Sex*, a book on gender research published in 1991: "Many women in the last thirty or forty years have been brought up to believe that they are, or should be, 'as good as the next man.'. . . Instead, in spite of greater emancipation in terms of education, opportunity, and social attitudes, women are not noticeably 'doing better' than they were thirty years ago."

What's holding women back, the authors argue, is not sex discrimination, but sex hormones: "To reconstruct the world on non-sexist lines takes a positive effort, because it is an unnatural act; it is a social and political precept, but political and social precepts do not organise [sic] brains. Only hormones do that."

If gender research is so biased and most of it doesn't apply to your child anyway, what's the point of reading up on it? There are several reasons. One reason is that the research has gotten better. As the world has become more sensitive to sexism, gender research has become more objective and more complex and interesting. The second reason is that even if individual findings don't seem relevant to your child, taken as a whole they provide a framework that you can use to gain some insights into your child and the company he or she keeps. Third, staying apprised of the research can help you recognize the gender stereotypes that may linger in your community. For example, are there teachers who act as though they think girls are better than boys at writing or that boys are better than girls at math? If so, then you need to act to make sure that your child doesn't get an inferior education because of gender biases at school.

Much of the research is about how you, the nurturer, affect your child. The key question is no longer, Is it nature or nurture? We know that it's nature *and* nurture. The question is how do nature and nurture interact to make girls and boys different in some ways and similar in others? There's little doubt that sex hormones shape the brain of a developing fetus one way if it's a boy and another way if it's a girl and that sex differences in the brain have something to do with sex differences in behavior; temperament; interests; and, in some cases, even health. But it's also clear that biology isn't destiny. A child's experiences also shape his or her brain, behavior, temperament, and the rest.

Even though gender research has improved, its reputation still suffers from its tainted past. "It's politically incorrect to talk about gender differences," said Kaveri Subrahmanyam, an assistant professor of child development at Cal State University in Los Angeles who studies gender differences in computer use. "You get a lot of flack in the scientific field for finding them."

No one has born the brunt of this flack more than the team of Yale doctors whose landmark research showed that women and men use their brains differently when reading. Their research opens up the possibility—but doesn't show—that males and females may have fundamentally unequal language skills. Still, when these doctors speak at conferences, they are heckled and jeered by some scientists. By the same token, there are doctors and female sports advocates who are uncomfortable with the recent findings that female athletes are especially vulnerable to knee injuries. It's not that these people dispute the evidence, but they are concerned that publicizing it could be bad for female athletes. The fear is that the high rate of knee injuries may be used to justify turning back the clock and eroding the gains that girls and women have made in sports.

Subrahmanyam speaks for several of the researchers and parents who were interviewed for this book when she says that it's time to move beyond the fear that finding sex differences will inevitably cause sex bias. "We'd be much better off to acknowledge differences and then find ways to work with them or use our knowledge of them to help boys and girls do better," she said. So, let's begin.

1

In the Beginning

Gender Differences in the Womb and in the First Two Years of Life

SEX MATTERS

Expectant parents can't help themselves. Long before their baby arrives, they're mentally cloning their child from one germ of information: the sex. If they know the sex of their baby from prenatal testing, their imagination can proceed along a story line that's laced with either pink or blue, barrettes or suspenders, ballet recitals or hockey camp. If they don't know the sex, they can create two story lines and make themselves giddy by fantasizing about the possibilities. Either way, the baby's "prequel" comes laden with assumptions about boys and girls, like who cries more; who sleeps better; and who's sweeter, more willful, tougher, more vulnerable, more active, easier, and maybe even more interesting.

"Do you know what you're having?" a guest asked Marie, the hostess of the party, who was six months pregnant with her third child and the mother of a 6-year-old girl and a 4-year-old boy.

"A girl," she beamed. "Thank God."

"Why do you say that?"

"Because girls are so much easier." Marie went on to say that her son was much more demanding than his older sister. He was colicky as an infant, and as a toddler and preschooler, he would vent his anger by hitting, pushing, and yelling. Marie also felt that her son needed more affection. "He was so clingy. He'd be all over me," she said. "I didn't understand him. My daughter wasn't like that."

Sue, the mother of two boys who was expecting her third child, explained why she wanted to know the sex of this baby ahead of time. "I needed to be prepared if I was having another boy," she said. But, she added with a smile, "It's a girl."

Not everyone thinks boys are trouble. When Vanessa was pregnant with her second child, she hoped for another boy because she thought *they* were easier. She based this impression on her relatively trouble-free experience with her 2-year-old son and, as a counterpoint, her difficult relationship with her mother. "With girls, you have all that mother-daughter stuff," she said. Another reason she didn't want a girl is that she didn't want to have to deal with the Barbies, frilly dresses, and other accessories that she considered trappings of prefeminist times but assumed most girls still wanted.

Everyone has an opinion on the differences between boys and girls. People may not agree on what those differences are, but they do agree on one thing—that boys and girls behave differently from the time they're babies. For years, scientists debunked that idea on the ground that infants were too young, too sexless, too clean a slate to show gender-specific traits. The only differences between boy and girl babies, they argued, were the ways that parents and other adults treated them.

Scientists had several "Baby X" studies to support the view that the difference between babies is in the eye of the beholder. These were studies in which adults were asked to describe or play with a baby that they thought was a boy but was really a girl, and vice versa. In some cases, the baby was dressed in girl's clothing for one group of adults and in boy's clothing for another group. In other cases, the baby was dressed in neutral clothing (like a yellow jumpsuit), and some of the adults were told that the baby was a boy, while others were told it was a girl. Regardless of the setup, the result was the same. The adults reacted to the babies differently, depending on whether they thought the babies were boys or girls. They'd offer the "girls" dolls, for instance, and the "boys" balls. In one study, in which an infant cried when startled by a jack-in-the-box, the adults who thought the baby was a boy interpreted the crying as a sign of anger, and the adults who thought the baby was a girl interpreted it as a sign of fear. This finding was proof, scientists said, that adults imagine differences between baby boys and girls on the basis of gender stereotypes.

It's certainly true that many of the ways that adults treat children are colored by stereotypes and that stereotypes can become self-fulfilling prophecies. But lately scientists have come around to the view that babies aren't clean slates after all. Some studies show what parents have assumed all along: that boys and girls behave slightly differently soon after birth. And with the advent of brain-imaging technology, scientists have been able to see differences in the brains of babies as young as 6 month old.

This chapter begins with the time and place where sex differences first show up in an embryo. Then it lays out the gender differences in behavior and development from birth until age 2—for example, how content or fussy female and male babies are and how quickly they reach key developmental milestones. Some of the scientific observations will no doubt confirm many parents' observations about their own sons and daughters, while others will challenge certain stereotypes about baby boys and girls.

The chapter goes on to discuss how some of the differences

in the ways that girls and boys act and develop relate to differences in their brains. At this point, no one knows exactly how gender-based variations in the brain translate into things like temperament, preferences for toys, and skills as a child grows. But differences in areas of the brain that appear to influence specific behaviors have led scientists to make some plausible, if still tentative, connections.

A biological predisposition is not destiny, however. How you and other caregivers treat your sons and daughters can either amplify or reduce their tendencies to develop in gender-typed ways. There's nothing wrong with boys and girls behaving differently or being treated differently, of course, unless it means that their opportunities for development are unequal. The suggestions for parents at the end of the chapter are things you can do to help prevent gender stereotypes from hindering your sons' and daughters' growth during the first two years of life.

THE SCIENCE OF SEXUAL DEVELOPMENT

Most pregnant women have this experience: Friends or even strangers say to a woman that they can "tell" whether she is carrying a boy or a girl. If she has bad morning sickness, if she grows wider throughout her body (not just around her middle), and if she carries high, people say that the baby is a girl. If her weight gain appears "all in the belly" and if she carries low, they say it's a boy. Whether these old wives' tales have any basis in reality is questionable, but the point is that sex matters so much that long before a baby is born, people are looking for clues to whether it is a boy or a girl.

As the due date draws closer, some women think that they can tell the sex of their baby according to the nature of its movements. In one study, women who were carrying boys described the fetal movements as "vigorous," "very strong," and "a saga of earthquakes." One mother referred to her unborn son as "the John Wayne fetus." Mothers who were carrying girls described their movements as "very gentle," "not terribly active," and "not violent." However, all these women knew their babies' sex from prenatal testing, so their opinions might well have been biased. In another study, in which the mothers did not know the sex of their fetuses, there was no correlation between the mothers' descriptions of the fetuses' movements and the babies' sex. Scientists' observations are mixed, too. Some scientists who have measured fetal movements report that male fetuses do indeed move around more than female fetuses, but others see no relationship between a fetus's sex and its activity level.

There is one symptom of pregnancy that really does seem to indicate the sex of the baby with reasonable accuracy. Asthmatic women who are carrying girls find that their asthma gets worse, whereas asthmatic women who are carrying boys find that their asthma either gets better or stays the same. The British doctors who discovered this association chalked it up to the different mix of sex hormones in the womb occupied by a male versus a female. Sex hormones affect the airways—asthma is worse in girls than in boys after puberty, when the differences in the levels of sex hormones become significant—but just how they do so is unknown. What *is* known are the many differences that hormones create in the developing embryo.

At first, there are surprisingly few differences. In the early weeks of gestation, male and female embryos look identical. They start out with the basic structures of both male and female sex organs. There are just two differences between the embryos. One, naturally, is in the sex chromosomes. Males have a pair of XY chromosomes, and females have a pair of XX chromosomes.

One X chromosome always comes from the mother's egg, but it is the father's sperm, which can carry either an X or a Y chromosome, that determines the baby's sex. If an X-bearing sperm fertilizes the egg, the baby is a girl; if a Y-bearing chromosome does the job, it's a boy.

The second difference between male and female embryos is numerical. More males are conceived. In the United States, the ratio is about 120 males to every 100 females. The reason may be related to the average frequency of intercourse: Studies suggest that the more often a couple has sex, the greater the odds of having a boy. And when couples are trying to conceive, it makes sense that they would have sex often.

As the weeks pass, a third difference emerges. More male fetuses die in miscarriages. No one knows why, but there are several theories. One is that they're more vulnerable to damage from the mother's or father's exposure to environmental pollutants. Another theory is that the sex difference between the mother and the male fetus may account for some of the risk. The mother's immune system may consider a male fetus to be more foreign than a female fetus and therefore may sometimes mistake a male fetus for a dangerous invader, like a bacteria or virus, and then attack it with antibodies.

Survival statistics aside, the first in a long and complex web of events that will ultimately influence differences in the ways that boys and girls look, behave, feel, and think occurs around the sixth week of gestation. This is the time when the male chromosome issues the command for the development of male gonads, and the pair of what had been neutral sex glands is transformed into testes. Oddly enough, there does not seem to be a parallel command from the female chromosome. As far as anyone can tell, it is the absence of information from the female chromosome that prompts the neutral sex glands to become ovaries, a phenomenon that has earned females the reputation in scientific circles for being the "default" sex. In a female fetus, the gonads wait for a signal from the female chromosome suspended in their bisexual state until the 12th week of gestation. If the signal doesn't come, the gonads develop as ovaries.

Sex hormones secreted by the ovaries and the testes influence the development of all the physical traits and, in all likelihood, many of the behavioral ones that set males and females apart. We tend to think in terms of "male" hormones and "female" hormones, but in fact this notion is misleading. All the sex hormones circulate through both males and females. The difference is a matter of degree. Males have higher levels of testosterone and other androgens. Females have higher levels of estrogen and progesterone.

If androgen levels are high enough, the penis develops and the parts of the female reproductive tract wither and disintegrate. If androgens are relatively low, the vagina, Fallopian tubes, and uterus grow and the male reproductive tract dies. But sex hormones influence more than just the developing reproductive organs. They also seem to play a role in sculpturing the brain.

SEX IN THE BRAIN

Certain brain structures and functions are different in males and females, and one reason for this difference appears to be the relative levels of androgens and estrogen bathing the fetus. Most of the male-female variations that have been found so far are in the hypothalamus, a relay station in the front-center of the brain that directs many sensations and operations in the body, including sexual arousal, hunger, thirst, and temperature regulation. Studies show that one minuscule bundle of nerves of the hypothalamus is five to eight times larger in male rats than in female rats. Because of the pronounced male-female difference, this area of the brain is called the sexually dimorphic nucleus, or SDN. In experiments in which baby male rats are deprived of testosterone, the SDN quickly shrinks.

Whether the SDN is also larger in human males than in human females is a matter of debate. Some studies say yes, others say no. But there is little doubt that there is a difference in a pin-prick-size cluster of cells located near the SDN. The INAH–3 (for the third interstitial nuclei of the anterior hypothalamus) has two and a half to three times more nerve cells in men than in women. The INAH–3 is the same size in male and female babies, but it begins to get bigger in boys when they're about 10. Scientists think that the INAH–3 is involved in regulating sexual desire. A study that made headlines in 1991 found that heterosexual men have more INAH–3 cells than do homosexual men, suggesting that homosexuality is a biological trait.

Undoubtedly, the most talked-about difference between male and female brains is the size of the nerve fibers that connect the right and left hemispheres. This bundle of fibers, called the corpus collosum, is larger in females than in males, which could explain differences in the ways that males and females think. Girls and women tend to use both sides of the brain at the same time when engaged in certain tasks, whereas boys and men tend to use just one side at a time.

A third difference is that the two hemispheres of the brain develop at different rates in girls and boys. The left hemisphere, the one that does most of the language processing, comes into use earlier in females. The right hemisphere, which specializes in certain spatial tasks, such as imagining how objects look from different angles or finding your way around a city, starts running earlier in males.

Some evidence linking sex differences in the brain with sex hormone levels in the womb comes from a study of women whose mothers used the drug DES (diethylstilbestrol) during pregnancy. DES, which was used from the 1940s to the 1970s to prevent miscarriages, is a curious substance because it's a synthetic estrogen that acts like an androgen in the body. In the study, "DES daughters" listened to a series of statements while scientists used brain-imaging machinery to see which regions of the brain were at work. The women whose mothers had not taken DES and had been exposed to normal levels of estrogen and androgens in utero tended to use both sides of the brain at once, the female pattern. But the women whose mothers had taken DES had more lateralized brain activity, the male pattern.

Listing the differences between males' and females' brains makes for engaging talk at the playground. But what do the differences really mean? What influence do prenatal hormones and differences in brain structure and functioning have in the months and years ahead, when girls play dress-up and boys run in packs across the playground? How much of a boy's and a girl's sense of self is encoded in the brain fibers and neurons at birth, and how much depends on the information that they process after birth: that mixed bag of "nurture" that includes the color of the bedroom walls; the selection of toys in the crib; the clothing the child wears; and, not the least, the parents' love and expectations?

Psychologists and neurologists will be busy for many years trying to tease out the answers. No one knows the relative importance of nature and nurture in charting a child's overall development. But a recent finding suggests that at least where gender identity—the sense of being a boy or a girl—is concerned, nature is more powerful than nurture.

The finding comes from research on the rare babies who have

what doctors delicately call "ambiguous genitalia"—that is, a penis that could be mistaken for a clitoris or a clitoris that looks somewhat like a penis. About 1 in 1,000 babies are born with chromosomal or hormone defects that prevent the sex organs from developing properly. Far rarer still are males whose penises are destroyed accidentally by circumcision and other kinds of surgery. In both cases, the standard medical practice for decades has been for doctors and parents to play God and assign the child a sex.

The doctor would operate on the genitals to make them look more normal, which usually meant fashioning a vagina, since constructing a penis is more difficult. The doctor would also inject the child with estrogen or testosterone at puberty to promote male or female sexual characteristics. The parents' role was to raise the child to be the chosen sex. If that sex was female, the parents would buy dresses and dolls and indoctrinate the child into the world of stereotypical female behavior. If the sex was male, the parents would buy trucks and footballs and teach the child how to be a boy.

One would be hard pressed to find a more extreme practice based on the long-standing conviction that the main difference between boys and girls is how they're treated. Studies following children who had sex-change operations and therapy show mixed results; many of the children accepted their assigned sex, others did not. But the practice of sexual reassignment was called into question a few years ago when the child who had been hailed as its greatest success story was revealed, on long-term follow-up, to have been its ultimate failure.

Bruce Reimer was born a healthy boy with a twin brother, but when he was 8 months old, his penis was cut off accidentally during a circumcision. Some months later, his genitals were surgically fashioned into a vagina, and his name was changed to Brenda. Brenda's parents bought her dresses and dolls. They sent her to female psychiatrists to help promote a female identity. But none of these efforts worked. Brenda refused to wear dresses. She played with boys rather than girls. She saved her allowance so she could buy a truck of her own, since her twin brother wouldn't share his trucks with her. She would even try to urinate standing up. As a teenager, despite estrogen injections, Brenda never felt sexually attracted to boys. She had no friends. Her classmates tormented her. She was so miserable, she considered suicide.

At 14, Brenda refused to take any more estrogen and openly questioned her female identity. At this point, her father told her about her history. But instead of causing anguish, the news came as a relief. "For the first time everything made sense," Brenda, as quoted in the study, said, "and I understood who and what I was."

Brenda/Bruce took male hormone injections and underwent several operations to return to his original sex. At 25, he married a woman. And, most important, he has said that he is happy as a man.

Of course, most children aren't like Bruce. Their sex isn't changed, so nature and nurture work in tandem to forge their gender identity. But when nature and nurture are at odds, Bruce's case suggests that nature rules. Medicine made Bruce look like a girl and people told him he was a girl, but no amount of "nurture" could convince his most important sex organ: his brain.

The prevailing view in gender research is that exposure to different levels of sex hormones before birth somehow primes males' and females' brains to develop and respond in different ways. If this is the case, then it stands to reason that there could be differences in the behavior of boys and girls as soon as they're born.

BOYS AND GIRLS AT BIRTH

As newborns, Kristen's son and daughter were as different as can be. Louis, the oldest, was extremely fussy. He would cry the moment he woke up. He barely slept at night. Maddy, two years younger, was the quintessential easy baby. She slept for longer stretches, and when she woke up, she would lie quietly looking around, content to wait to be picked up and nursed. Kristen wonders how much the differences between Louis and Maddy are due to their personalities and how much—if any—to their sex. Are newborn girls in general more easygoing?

There are differences between boys and girls that reveal themselves at birth, although they're not necessarily the ones that parents expect. The first difference sometimes shows up during labor. Women who are having her first baby spend over an hour and a half longer in labor with a son than with a daughter, even if their pregnancies were trouble-free. Newborn boys weigh about 5 percent more than newborn girls, and heavier babies are harder to deliver. But even when the weight difference is accounted for, boys still take longer to be born for some reason. And there's a snowball effect. The longer the labor, the more likely that the baby will have complications or suffer trauma, which can make the baby fussier and more wakeful in the days and weeks ahead.

From the time they're born, boys are at a greater risk of health problems. In what is perhaps the most extensive study of gender differences in the health of children, the government of Finland tracked all children born in 1987 and followed them for nine years. It found that the boys had a 20 percent greater risk of a low five-minute Apgar score, a standard assessment of health based on an evaluation of heart rate, breathing, muscle tone, reflexes, and skin tone done five minutes after birth. No doubt, one reason is that the boys were 11 percent as likely to be born prematurely, itself a risk factor for poor health. In the seven years after birth, the boys had a 22 percent greater risk of dying, a 64 percent higher incidence of asthma, and a 43 percent higher incidence of intellectual disabilities. They were two to three times as likely as girls to have developmental delays that caused to them either to start school late or to need special education.

Smaller studies in the United States have reached the same general conclusion: Boys are more vulnerable than girls. Infant sons of diabetic mothers are twice as likely as infant daughters to die or be disabled as a result of the effects of their mothers' illness on the pregnancies. Premature girls have greater odds for survival than premature boys. My friend Marilyn suffered complications with her third pregnancy that caused her to give birth seven weeks early to a baby weighing less then 2 pounds. Soon after delivery, when the baby arrived in the neonatal intensive care unit, her survival was in question: She could stop breathing in an instant, and any of her organs could fail. But with it all, the nurses and doctors told Marilyn and Max that they were lucky for no reason other than that they'd had a girl.

This is a standard line that doctors and nurses give to parents of newborn girls who need intensive care, said Pat Bruceson, a nurse with the National Association of Neonatal Nurses. Parents of girls are lucky because girls are hardier and more resilient. Bruceson said that roughly the same number of premature boys and girls come into hospital neonatal intensive care units, but far more girls survive and eventually go home. About three months after she was born, Marilyn's and Max's baby Thelma went home, leaving the intensive care unit full of mostly girls.

Just why boys are more physically vulnerable has puzzled scientists for many years. One theory is that boys' brains are more easily damaged before, during, and after birth because boys' nervous systems are less mature than girls' at birth. The less mature the nervous system, the more fragile it is. Another possible explanation is that male infants are more easily stressed. In experiments in which researchers exposed infants to a mild but prolonged stressful event, the boys' levels of cortisol, a stress hormone in the blood, shot up, whereas the girls' cortisol stayed the same. Increased cortisol can suppress immune function as well as growth hormones. Testosterone may also make males more vulnerable, since it, too, lowers immune function.

Who's Easier? Who's Fussier?

Despite newborn boys' greater medical and developmental risks, boys and girls in this country who are born full term without complications look more similar than different. You can't tell them apart as newborns by their hearing and vision tests, eye movements, senses of smell, and metabolisms (although boys' metabolisms start to run higher later in infancy). And since the boys' and girls' senses are equally keen, scientists have long thought that their actions and reactions were more or less the same, too at least in the first two years of life.

Recently, doctors have taken a closer look at the behavior of boys and girls in the weeks, days, and even hours after birth. Traits found so early are especially significant because they are least likely to be influenced by the stereotypical ways that parents and other people treat baby girls and boys. T. Berry Brazelton, the noted pediatrician and author, is one of the doctors who has found that within hours of delivery, girls seem more social than boys in the sense that they maintain eye contact for a longer time and are more responsive to other people and to sounds. Some studies have also found that girls are calmer and cry less than do boys and that when they do cry, they're more apt to calm themselves down. Although girls seem to be calmer and quieter, they don't necessarily sleep for longer stretches. Richard Ferber, a Harvard neurologist and the author of *Solve Your Child's Sleep Problems*, has not found that baby boys have more difficulty getting to sleep and staying asleep than do baby girls.

As with virtually all the differences between groups of boys and groups of girls, those seen at birth are smaller than the differences between any two girls or boys. My son, David, was extremely fussy. My daughter, Sarah, was much more easygoing, and their cousin Michele was far more so. I can recall Michele lying in her cradle while the family ate an uninterrupted dinner—something that neither of my children would do. My friend Maura's son, Will, was like Michele.

If newborn boys as a group are fussier, it may have less to do with their basic nature than with their early life experiences. In addition to enduring longer, more traumatic deliveries, many baby boys undergo circumcision, a minor operation to remove the foreskin of the penis that, until recently, was routinely done without painkillers. Circumcised boys tend to be fussier than girls or uncircumcised boys in the week or so after their operation for the understandable reason that they are in more pain. But the jury is out on the relative fussiness of girls and uncircumcised boys. In one study that compared uncircumcised 2-day-old boys with 2-day-old girls—and matched the babies for length of labor and exposure to pain medicine—the boys still cried more and were generally more irritable. But other studies have not found this difference.

At this point, it's impossible to say whether a baby's sex predicts how easy or difficult he or she will be during the newborn period, in the first month of life. Some factors associated with boys, like a difficult delivery or circumcision, can make them more irritable in the beginning. But what happens to baby boys and girls in the months and years ahead? Are there things that parents do inadvertently to turn small, subtle differences between newborn boys and girls into larger ones?

HOW PARENTS TREAT THEIR SONS AND DAUGHTERS

Even if parents could train themselves to disregard all the gender stereotypes, it would stand to reason that they'd treat their sons and daughters differently. Given that boys and girls behave somewhat differently soon after birth, they elicit different reactions from their parents. This is not to say that parents play favorites. Studies have looked at things like how quickly parents respond to their babies' cries and how affectionate parents are with their children, and they've found no differences in the amount of love and attention parents give their sons and daughters.

But differences have been noted in the ways that parents *show* their love and attention. As early as the first weeks of their babies' lives, parents spend more time socializing with their daughters than with their sons. They look into their daughters' eyes, smile, and talk to them. It's possible that conversation strikes some parents as an appropriate "girl" activity, fitting with the stereotype that girls like to talk (even before they know how). It's also likely that parents talk to girls more because they're easier to talk to. In those early weeks, baby girls tend to hold a person's gaze longer and spend slightly more time alert and content than boys do. In this state, they practically invite parents to cradle them in their arms, smile, coo, and talk to them.

Parents are also more protective of their daughters, perhaps because of the stereotype that baby girls are more delicate than baby boys. Research shows that parents hover over their daughters more than their sons, especially once the daughters become mobile and are able to do things like climb the playground ladder. Some studies have also found that parents are quicker to rush to their daughters' aid when they're becoming frustrated with a new task, be it working the busy box in their cribs or stacking blocks.

While parents give their sons no less attention, researchers have found that they spend less of it in face-to-face communication. Instead of talking and gazing, they're more apt to roughhouse with their sons, perhaps because they think that baby boys can (or should be able to) handle it. Roughhousing with a newborn can mean moving his arms and legs or tickling him or speaking to him in a playfully gruff tone of voice. Parents also spend more time trying to console their infant sons because, due to the pain from circumcision and their increased incidence of birth trauma, baby boys tend to cry more. To calm their sons down, parents inevitably find themselves carrying them over their shoulders and rocking them or walking them back and forth, not communicating with them face-to-face.

As the months pass, this pattern of parent-child interaction continues. Boys cry more, become upset more easily, and stay upset longer than do girls. It's not that girls don't cry to be picked up and rocked. They're babies, after all. But by the time they're 6 months old, girls need less attention. They're more likely than boys to suck their thumbs and look at toys for consolation, while boys are still looking to their parents and other caregivers.

It can't be circumcision pain that's making the boys cranky, since the pain has long since subsided by the time they're several months old. Then what's going on? Did parents spoil their sons by spending a lot of time rocking and walking with them early on? Or are their sons really needier?

VULNERABLE BOYS

Aside from being more vulnerable physically than girls, it appears that boys are also more vulnerable emotionally. Things that normally upset a baby, like a change of routine or a harsh tone of voice from Mom or Dad, upset boys more. Not all boys, perhaps not *your* boy. But more boys than girls.

A series of experiments at Harvard tracked emotional vulnerability in baby boys and girls. M. Katherine Weinberg, a researcher at Harvard Medical School, and her colleagues wanted to see if infant boys really did become more agitated in response to a stressful experience. The researchers also wanted to see if the boys' mothers behaved differently than the girls' mothers did. To find out, the researchers videotaped 6-month-old babies in the laboratory as they sat in infant seats and played with their mothers. First, their mothers showed them toys and talked with them. Then, for two minutes, the mothers stopped playing and assumed an emotionless "still-face" expression, which was intended to upset the babies. Afterward, the researchers played back the videotape in extremely slow motion to analyze the fraction-of-a-second changes in the babies' and mothers' expressions and behavior. Sure enough, the boys cried and fussed more, looked angrier, and either gestured to the mothers that they wanted be picked up or squirmed in their infant seats as if they were trying to get away.

After the still-face experiment was over, the mothers did what they could to soothe their babies—touched them, talked to them, and gazed at them. There was no difference in the strategies that the mothers used with their sons as opposed to daughters. But it took the boys longer to calm down. And even when the boys were calm, they spent more time vying for their mothers' attention by looking at them and vocalizing to them. The girls, by contrast, focused less on their mothers than on the toys scattered around them. The girls didn't need their mothers as much for help in calming down when they were upset, and they didn't need to check in with their mothers as much during times when they were content. What this finding suggests, the researchers said, is that "mothers and sons may need to work harder than mothers and daughters in keeping the interaction affectively well organized." In other words, it takes more effort to make infant boys happy.

Baby boys demand more from their parents because they seem to need more. Study after study indicates that boys are more emotionally vulnerable than girls. It's not that parents train their sons to be dependent on them by indulging them with attention. In the Harvard study, the mothers didn't treat the sons and daughters differently. But it does appear that parents who withhold attention from their sons, perhaps in an attempt to toughen them up or to avoid spoiling them, can do them great harm.

An extreme example comes from a study done by Nancy Bayley, the researcher who developed the Bayley Scales, assessments used to track developmental milestones in children from birth to age 3. In the 1960s, Bayley compared 18-month-old babies whose mothers were so severely depressed that they were withdrawn or hostile with another group whose mothers were not depressed. Then, when the children were 3 to 5 years old, she gave them intelligence tests. A child's level of intelligence is usually similar to that of his or her biological parents, since intelligence is partly inherited. It is also influenced by the socioeconomic class of the child's household—the higher the family's social class and income, generally speaking, the higher a child's intelligence.

In Bayley's study, the scores of the boys with the depressed mothers were lower than the scores of the other boys and were lower than expected on the basis of their mothers' intelligence and the household's socioeconomic class. The scores of the girls with the depressed mothers were not lower than expected. But another group of girls did have unusually low scores: girls whose mothers were overprotective, shielding them from experiences to explore and learn. So, the boys' intelligence suffered from too little affection, and the girls' suffered from too much.

Even in less dire circumstances, boys are more vulnerable to problems stemming from a lack of affection. Numerous studies have found that boys who have emotionally distant relationships with their parents are more likely than girls in this situation to have behavioral problems and trouble getting along with peers in preschool. Laura Allen, a neuroscientist who has studied sex differences in the brain at UCLA, has a theory that for boys more than for girls, affection may actually help shape the brain by altering levels of androgens. She bases this theory on evidence from studies of rats. But her impression that boys are more emotionally fragile than girls comes not just from being a scientist but from being a parent. "My little girl adapted better to baby-sitters and was more adaptable in general than my son," she said.

Her children aren't the only ones. A National Institutes of Health study followed 1,300 families from the time the children were 1 month old until they were in elementary school to examine the effects of child care on the families. One of the many things that the researchers measured was the bond between the mothers and the children, long considered a prime indicator of a young child's emotional well-being. A child who is securely attached to a parent will show it by looking happy when the parent walks in the door after having been away for several hours, whereas a child who is insecurely attached will often frown, look away, or even move away from the parent.

When the children in the study were 18 months old, the researchers found a small but significant difference between girls and boys whose mothers worked at least 30 hours a week and those who worked fewer than 10 hours. That is, 58 percent of the boys whose mothers worked the longer hours were securely attached, compared with 65 percent of the boys whose mothers worked the shortest hours. Curiously, the numbers were reversed for the girls: 66 percent of the daughters of mothers who worked the most were securely attached and just 58 percent of the daughters whose mothers worked shorter hours or didn't work were securely attached.

Although the findings add further evidence that boys are a bit less emotionally resilient than girls, they should not be taken to mean that mothers of sons should quit their jobs—or, for that matter, that mothers of daughters should work longer hours, said Jay Belsky, one of the researchers. For one thing, the difference in attachment between the children whose mothers worked the most and the least hours was very small. And the study found that a far stronger influence on attachment was how the mothers spent their time with their children. The mothers who were loving and responsive forged strong bonds with their children, regardless of the children's sex and how many hours they spent away from home.

DO GIRLS MATURE FASTER?
MYTHS AND FACTS

At this point, it's easy to come away with the impression that girls are the stronger sex. Faced with medical adversity at birth, they're more likely to survive. By the time they're 6 months old, they're more independent in the sense that they don't need as much from their caregivers, and their emotional and cognitive well-being doesn't depend as much on the quality of their relationship with their parents. Again, it must be stressed that the differences are slim. Your infant son may be easygoing and resourceful, while your daughter may be the one who bawls when the lights are too bright or the music is too loud. But in any case, the gender differences seen so far don't suggest that baby girls are inherently more miraculous, astonishing, lovable, or better in any way than baby boys. What they really come down to are biological differences in the rate at which boys and girls mature.

Everyone says that girls mature faster than boys, and it's true—partially. Girls don't do everything first. When scientists speak of maturation, they mean the whole spectrum of physical, cognitive, emotional, and social development. There are the inches grown and pounds gained; the cutting of teeth; and the achievement of milestones, such as rolling over, sitting up, walking, talking, and using utensils like spoons and forks. No two children do any of these things at the same pace. And no single child matures at the same rate in all areas; for example, a child may talk early and walk late. In most respects, boys and girls as groups mature at the same rate. But there are some important exceptions.

Girls are more physically mature than boys even before they're born. Halfway through gestation, girls' bone development is three weeks ahead of boys'. At birth, girls are four- to six weeks ahead in this regard, and by the time they reach puberty, their bone development is two years ahead of boys'. The same difference is seen in most primates and many other mammals. Infant boys and girls cut their teeth during the same range of months, but girls get their permanent teeth earlier—as much as

11 months earlier in the case of the canine teeth. Girls reach half their adult height, enter puberty, and stop growing earlier than do boys.

By the time they're 7 months old, even though many girls and boys are rolling over, sitting up, and possibly even crawling, girls are way ahead in fine motor skills like manipulating infant spoons and forks, making strike marks with crayons, and pulling zippers. This difference lasts for many years. Linda Jo Platt, the director of Community Nursery School in Dobbs Ferry, New York, has observed that the 3-year-old girls in her school are about six months ahead the 3-year-old boys in fine motor skills. And in elementary school, girls usually have better penmanship, although it's hard to say whether their penmanship is better only because they have better control over the pencil or because they care more about forming their letters properly.

Girls' superior fine motor skills have been recognized for decades by scientists (longer, no doubt, by parents and teachers). Scientists think that the gender difference must correspond to some anatomic or functional difference in boys' and girls' brains that is shaped by sex hormones during prenatal development. But just what that difference *is* has yet to be identified. Some sex differences in the brain have been found, however, that seem to explain two other areas in which girls mature faster than boys: language development and self-control.

Language

Girls begin to talk earlier than boys. In one study, half the 10-month-old girls were saying three words and half the boys that age were saying one word. At 16 months, half the girls had a vocabulary of 56 words, whereas half the boys said just 28 words. The girls understood more words, too. In the same evaluation, half the 10-month-old girls indicated through their responses that they understood 46 words, whereas half the boys indicated that they understood 39 words. This difference was so slight that it might have been dismissed as a fluke or an error, except that it got larger with age. At 16 months, half the girls understood 206 words and half the boys understood only 134 words. It wasn't until they were 20 months old that boys comprehended as many words as girls. But even then and in the years to come, research shows girls talk more and make fewer mispronunciations and other mistakes in their speech.

Several characteristics of girls' brains probably give girls a verbal edge. One is that as babies, girls use the left hemisphere of the brain earlier than boys do. The left hemisphere is the half of the brain that does most of the work of processing language. Girls also have more tightly packed neurons in areas in both sides of the brain that process language. Janet and David Shucard, neurologists at the University of Buffalo, measured electrical activity in the brains of 3 month olds as they listened to someone talking. The girls processed the sounds in the left hemisphere, the boys in the right hemisphere. When the Shucards repeated the experiment with 6 month olds, the boys were still processing the language sounds in the right hemisphere. It wasn't until the boys were 9 months old that they finally began to use the left hemisphere. What this experiment suggests is that at 6 months, girls are laying down a lot more language information in their brains than boys are.

It's unlikely that biology is the only reason why girls have a way with words. Parents and other caregivers undoubtedly also play a role. For one thing, parents hold more "conversations" with their daughters. And talking promotes more talking, especially during the period from birth to age 3, when the brain is developing at a rapid clip. Research presented at a White House conference on child development in 1997 showed that the number of words spoken to an infant each day is the single most important predictor of the child's intelligence, academic success, and social abilities in the years ahead. It seems that talking, as well as seeing a variety of sights and hearing a variety of sounds, actually stimulates the nerve cells in the brain to connect up, laying the foundation for intelligence, creativity, and social adaptability.

Adults do other things to encourage girls to speak and discourage boys from speaking. In a provocative study, researchers at the Oregon Social Learning Center observed 13-month-old infants in playgroups to see how the boys and girls attempted to communicate with the caregivers and how the caregivers responded. In particular, the researchers wanted to know if the girls vocalized more than the boys or relied more on gestures, such as pointing, which are considered precursors of actual speech. And they watched to see if the boys relied more heavily on negative attention-getting techniques like whining, crying, or screaming.

In this study, the boys and girls made the same effort to communicate and used the same mix of techniques. The only differences were the caregivers' responses. The caregivers gave the girls the most attention when they babbled, said actual words, or used gestures. But they were most responsive to the boys when they whined, cried, screamed, or pulled on their clothing or hair.

About 11 months later, when the children were around 2 years old, the researchers watched most of the children in playgroups again. By then, the girls and boys did communicate differently. The girls talked more, and the boys used more disruptive attention-getting devices like shouting and hitting. The suggestion here is that the caregivers helped train the boys and girls to communicate differently. By responding more readily to verbal communication from girls, they rewarded the girls for trying to talk. And by responding more readily to negative non-verbal communication from boys, they discouraged them from talking. "By using the sex stereotype to guide their reactions to younger children, the caregivers may have perpetuated the stereotype," the researchers wrote.

Why the caregivers treated the boys and girls differently is anyone's guess. It could be that they were more likely to "hear" the girls speak because they expected the girls to be more verbal. In any case, the point of the study was not to single out child care providers and blame them for the differences in boys' and girls' language development, but simply to illustrate how they and other adults may behave in subtle ways that encourage girls to talk more. It's easy to imagine that the 13-month-old girls in the study went on to talk more at home, and so their parents kept up the flow of conversation. By contrast, the boys may have done more crying and fussing to get their parents' attention, prompting their parents to spend more time shouting, "No!" than engaging in the enjoyable verbal give-and-take that builds children's language skills.

The finding is a cautionary tale to parents because it shows how treating boys and girls differently may lead them to behave and develop differently. And given the evidence that talking to children may give them an edge in intelligence, creativity, and social smarts, parents and caregivers would be wise to talk more to boys. For parents whose infant son is a bit cranky, this means seizing the opportunity to have a little chat with him during those periods when he's awake and content. Whether talking more to boys will put their language skills on a par with girls' is an open question, but it certainly can't hurt.

Self-Control

All infants and toddlers get into trouble, especially once they become mobile. They're so intrigued by the lamp cord draped over the side of the table that they just have to crawl over and tug on it. They see people slipping things into the VCR, so it's only natural for them to stick their hand in to see what happens. And so on. But one of the biggest differences between boys and girls this age is that girls are more apt to learn from a mistake—either because they got hurt or because their parent said, "No!"—and stop themselves from making it again. In other words, they have more self-control.

Eleanor Maccoby, a psychologist at Stanford University and a pioneering researcher on gender development, has this vivid description of 1-year-old boys and girls in a doctor's waiting room. The boys reached for objects that their parents told them not to touch far more often than did the girls. By Maccoby's count, the parents—in this case, fathers—said, "No!" and "Stop it" and similar commands twice as often to the boys as to the girls. "It is surprising that boys should have been getting into mischief more often than girls at such an early age," Maccoby wrote in *The Two Sexes: Growing Up Apart, Coming Together.*

Of course, not all boys are naughtier than girls. Many parents would dispute that their sons are more mischievous than their daughters. And, let's face it, the child-proofing industry wasn't created only for boys. I remember the glee in my daughter's face when she was about 1 year old and toddled into the bathroom and started unraveling the toilet paper. I kept saying, "No," but she kept on going, turning her head from time to time to make sure I was watching. It was a game. She was misbehaving on purpose. All toddlers do so, but boys as a group do it more often and more persistently. They just don't seem to be able to control themselves.

Boys' relative lag in developing self-control can reveal itself in many other ways. Take, for example, a classic experiment that is designed to test infants' memory and impulse control. The experiment involves hiding an object in one place and then, while the infant watches, moving the object to another hiding place. Infants who are 8 months old and younger usually look for the object in its original place, a sign that they either forgot that they saw it moved to a new place or that they remembered but still could not resist the impulse to look in the first hiding place. In one study, male and female infants got better at this experiment as they got older, but the girls made the fastest progress.

A leading theory is that the areas of the brain's frontal lobes that control impulses develop more slowly in boys. Evidence comes from monkeys that were given the same experiment just described. The monkeys whose frontal lobes had been injured did not do as well on the experiment as the monkeys whose brains were intact. However, they did equally well on another task that tested only their memory, not their impulse control.

Whether it's the frontal lobes or some other area, real-life evidence suggests that *some* difference in brain maturation explains the difference in impulse control between boys and girls. Think of toilet training. This milestone isn't just a function of maturation below the belt; it's a sign of maturation above the neck, in the brain, in this case its ability to control the bladder and sphincter. As most parents discover, girls become toilet trained earlier than do boys. In one study, 30 percent of the girls and only 15 percent of the boys were trained by the time they were 2 1/2. At 3 years old, 70 percent of the girls and just slightly more than half the boys were toiled trained. Maccoby regards the gender difference in toilet training as a kind of yardstick of the brain's maturation.

Boys are slower to gain self-control in other respects. Tantrums are normal for all children from the ages of 1 to 2, but after around 2, girls begin to throw fewer of them. Boys don't. They're more emotional and more given to venting their anger, frustration, or despair. In day care or preschool, more often than not the child who hits another child or cries for longer than five minutes after Mom or Dad leave is a boy. "Any preschool director will tell you that 75 percent of the children who have trouble adjusting to preschool are boys," said Linda Jo Platt, who has more than three decades of experience teaching young children.

Over the years, Platt has found some techniques for smoothing boys' adjustment to preschool and even helping them mature in the areas where they are behind girls. For one thing, she thinks it's important for teachers not to force boys to join in all the organized activities if they're reluctant to do so because boys, due to their lag in self-control, have trouble sitting still and following instructions. Many boys are more comfortable playing on their own at first and joining in the organized activities when they're ready.

The presence of girls seems to help with the process, which is one reason why Platt makes a policy of having equal numbers of boys and girls in each class. Boys and girls learn by watching each other. Platt thinks that seeing the girls pay attention and listening to them talk helps the boys learn to pay attention and talk better. There's something in it for the girls, too. As the school year progresses, Platt sees them branching out physically and becoming more active in the presence of boys.

LEARNING STEREOTYPES

Many parents of young children face the first day of day care or preschool with mixed emotions. On the one hand, they welcome the opportunities that their children will have to socialize. On the other hand, they fear that their children will pick up bad habits, like aggressive behavior, or unsound ideas, like gender stereotypes. When Sam started day care at about age 2, his parents were happy with the caregivers, but less than thrilled that their son was coming home and talking about guns and pretending to shoot people.

Sam's parents were able to trace Sam's new behavior to several boys in his class. But Sam was probably picking up all sorts of gender stereotypes long before he fell in with this crowd. Contrary to what many parents think, the process of learning about gender stereotypes doesn't start in school. New research suggests that it starts when a baby is about 2 months old, and he or she can first tell the difference between a male voice and a female voice. From the moment that your baby starts to distinguish between males and females, he or she is absorbing tidbits of information about gender differences by touching you and by watching and listening to you and all the other people who come and go throughout the day.

Marie Driver Leinbach and her colleagues at the University of Oregon think that in a child's mind, all this sensory data is transformed into metaphors, the association of, say, deep voices with men and flowered dresses with women. These metaphors are building blocks of gender stereotypes. For example, a baby may notice that men have rough-sounding voices and rough-textured faces and link these qualities to form an impression of men as being rough. The baby may also notice that women have sweet voices and soft skin and come to associate these qualities with women. Any gender difference—in size, body contours, or movement patterns—can become the stuff of metaphors and then stereotypes. Most females are smaller than males, therefore small animals like butterflies are female. Males are large, so big animals like bears are male.

No one is proposing that infants are capable of such complex thinking. The theory is that they're collecting information, making associations, and filing them away for later use. My daughter may well have been accessing her database of metaphors when, at about age 3, she'd look at pictures of animals in books and call kittens and bunnies girls and large dogs and gorillas boys. In a study, Leinbach and her colleagues asked children ages 4 and older to sort various words according to whether they seemed boyish or girlish. Some words had obvious gender associations, like needle and thread and rifle. But others were metaphorical, like butterfly, feather, and round and bear, angular, and burlap. The majority of the children said that the first group of words—those representing soft or dainty qualities—was feminine and the second—representing large, hard-edged, and tough qualities—was masculine.

So, if the Oregon researchers' theory is true, it doesn't matter what color you paint your baby's room. By the time the child is old enough to show a preference for playing ball or playing dress-up, he or she will already think that boys are big, rough, and wild like bears and girls are small, delicate, and decorative like butterflies.

SUMMING UP

The differences between boys and girls are not just in the eye of the beholder. As infants, girls as a group are more alert and easily consoled. As the months pass, they tend to talk sooner, say more, and be more compliant. Boys are more fragile, medically as well as emotionally. They're more susceptible to birth defects and developmental disabilities. They're more vulnerable to the ill effects of an extreme lack of affection at home. They're more easily stressed, which means that they cry more when upset and have a harder time calming down.

This isn't to say that all boys are like boys *as a group* and all girls are like girls *as a group*. They're not. There's far more variation among individual girls and among individual boys than there is between boys and girls as groups. But boys and girls enter the world with a tendency to behave and develop somewhat differently.

It's not that boys are less desirable babies; their vulnerability and crying are signs of their immaturity relative to girls. At birth, girls' bones are four- to six weeks ahead of boys', and their brains are more highly developed, which probably affects things like how early they speak, how much they fuss for you to pick them up, and how well they listen when you say "No!" It isn't just that girls' and boys' brains mature at different rates; they are also different structurally. These differences, shaped by the levels of male and female sex hormones present in the womb, are thought to affect the children's behavior to some extent for their entire lives.

But boys and girls are more than just the sum of their biological parts. They're treated differently, and the ways that parents, caregivers, teachers, and other adults respond to them can amplify or mute their biological tendencies. Baby girls may get the language centers of their brains up and running before boys do, but parents and other adults also spend more time talking to girls. So, both nature and nurture help give them an edge verbally. We can't change nature, but tinkering with the nurture part of the equation can influence whether gender differences in language and other areas are great or small.

SUGGESTIONS FOR PARENTS

Even those of us who are intent on disregarding gender stereotypes about babies and toddlers may at times unwittingly treat young girls and boys in ways that reinforce such stereotypes and limit the children's opportunities for growth. Here are suggestions from researchers on gender development on ways that parents can meet the different needs of their sons and daughters in the first two years of life.

Give Your Son the Attention He Needs. Research suggests that infant boys need more attention than do infant girls. For example, they need more comforting to help them calm down when they're upset. But research also shows that many parents still hold back from giving their sons "too much" attention for fear of turning them into mamma's boys. Laura Allen, a neuroscientist who has done research on gender differences in the brain, thinks that such fear can have serious consequences. She notes that when deprived of affection, boys' intellectual development suffers more than girls', according to some studies.

Talk More to Your Son. Parents spend less time talking to their infant sons than to their infant daughters, a factor that may partially explain why boys talk later and then go on to talk less than girls. Research shows that regular, one-on-one conversations are among the most important factors for brain development, especially during the first three years of life when the brain is growing most rapidly. No study has demonstrated that talking more to boys will improve their language skills, but boys are bound to appreciate the attention.

Let Your Daughter Stumble. Girls' intellectual development suffers more than boys' when they get too much attention in the form of parental control. Some studies show that parents are quicker to help their daughters when they're struggling to do something than they are to help their sons, perhaps because of stereotypical notions that girls need to be protected from failure and boys need to play through the pain. But by shielding their daughters from failure, parents may be setting them up to fail. Both girls and boys benefit from being left to try, fail, and then keep trying until they succeed, whether they're learning to walk or to stack blocks. The experience builds confidence and self-reliance.

Get Your Son Working with His Hands. Boys' fine-motor skills lag behind girls'. The difference can be significant in school, when more boys than girls fumble with pencils as they learn to write. Researchers (and many parents) find that young boys are naturally drawn to gross-motor play, like throwing a ball or running, but they may need some gentle encouragement to try their hands at fine-motor activities, like drawing, stringing beads, and fitting together interlocking blocks. These activities can help develop a toddler's fine-motor skills.

Look for Gender Equity in Caregivers. You may be careful to avoid gender stereotypes with your children, but what about your nanny or the teachers at day care or preschool? When evaluating day care centers or group child care providers, watch to see that they don't encourage the girls and boys to engage in gender-typed activities. In addition, look for a degree of flexibility. Young boys may refuse to join group activities at first because they have more trouble than girls sitting still and following instruction, a function of their lag in self-control. An understanding caregiver will let such toddlers play on their own until they're ready to participate with the group.

In addition, look for signs that the caregivers are equally responsive to the boys and girls. Some research suggests that child care providers not only talk more to girls than to boys, but respond more readily to talk from girls. On the other hand, the research shows that caregivers give boys the most attention when they cry, hit, or behave in some other negative way. With their different responses, these caregivers may be discouraging boys from talking and encouraging them to use less desirable means of communication.

These kinds of comparisons are harder to make with a nanny unless there are a boy and a girl at home. Otherwise, you need to get a sense, through conversation and observation, of whether the nanny enjoys listening and talking to your child, regardless of your child's sex.

2

Boys, Girls, and Personality

Which Traits Are Gender Based?

BOYS WILL BE BOYS,
GIRLS WILL BE GIRLS

Huck Finn was adventurous, but are most boys like him? Little Miss Muffet was easily frightened, but are most girls fearful? In many storybooks, male and female characters have distinct temperamental characteristics, but is the same true for real boys and girls?

Much as parents want to think of their children as individuals, many can't help but wonder sometimes if certain personality traits really do cluster by sex. For example, when statistics tell us that boys and men commit most of the violent crimes, it's only natural to ask if males are more aggressive than females. When girls spend hours on the phone gossiping, it's hard not to suspect that females are fundamentally more social or, at least, cattier.

Then again, we tend to pay attention to the kinds of behavior that confirm our stereotypes about the true nature of boys and girls. Most boys aren't violent. Does this mean that the stereotype about boys being more aggressive than girls is wrong, or do most boys let out their aggression in other ways? Many girls today are too busy playing sports or pursuing other activities to dwell on their classmates' flaws. What do we make of these girls? Are they the exceptions to the catty-female stereotype, or do they disprove it?

Studies that have looked at gender and personality have found that most traits are not gender based. Neither sex has the lion's share of members who are optimistic or pessimistic, relaxed or nervous, sociable or reserved, patient or impatient, hostile or kind, and so on. There's more of a difference between individuals of either sex than between males and females. But there are a few exceptions. For example, studies do show that boys are more aggressive than girls. When researchers count how many times children hit, grab, and fight physically, the score is higher for boys than for girls.

But the gender difference in aggressiveness isn't as great as was once thought. The latest studies acknowledge that girls can be very aggressive. Now that researchers have broadened their definition of aggression to include fighting words, not only physical fighting, they're recognizing that girls and boys show aggression in different ways: Boys hit, and girls gossip.

This chapter is broken down into sections devoted to personality traits that are commonly associated with either boys or girls. Each section looks at the latest research on what, if any, gender differences have been found. When a personality characteristic does seem to be more prevalent among girls or boys, the section explores why. As with many of the gender differences in behavior, those associated with basic personality are thought to be related, in part, to male-female differences in the brain that, in all likelihood, arise from exposure to different levels of sex hormones before birth. But personality is also shaped by experience—the ways in which boys and girls are treated by their parents and others, as well as the examples of gender stereotypes they see in books, TV shows, and movies, as well as in playmates.

Much as they try to be objective, even scientists have a hard time studying gender differences in personality without falling into the same trap that parents fall into: picking out the behavior that confirms the gender stereotypes. Some of the published scientific findings read like self-fulfilling prophecies. Still, much of the research is illuminating for two reasons. In teasing out information about groups of children, it can help parents answer a question that they ask themselves over and over again: Is it just *my* kid? And since scientists, compared with the society as whole, find far fewer personality traits that are really more common in boys or in girls, the studies can move us closer to separating myth from fact.

A LOOK BACK

Today, if one parent casually mentions to another that girls are more social or boys are more active, the statement is unlikely to raise an eyebrow. But if those parents were to go back a quarter of a century and listen to parents—or researchers—speculating about possible gender differences in personality, they'd be in for a shock. In their groundbreaking 1974 book on gender development, *The Psychology of Sex Differences*, Eleanor Maccoby and Carol Nagy Jacklin set out to separate fact from stereotype by combing through all the gender literature to date and laying out what it said about the nature of boys and girls. The summary and commentary at the end is a kind of scorecard of traits that were thought at the time to be especially common in boys or in girls.

Many of the traits cited are the sorts of things that people still wonder about today: Are girls more nurturing? Are boys more competitive? But some of the supposedly gender-specific traits that were discussed back then reflect the greater gender bias of the time, especially the belief that girls' personalities made them intellectually inferior to boys. Girls were thought to be more suggestible than boys. They were also thought to be less motivated to achieve. And they were considered better suited to rote learning and simple repetitive tasks, while boys were thought to have the edge in tasks that require higher-level thinking. Related to boys' supposedly superior intellect was the assumption that they were more analytic, better able to home in on the relevant aspects of a task and avoid letting extraneous information get in the way.

Maccoby and Jacklin asserted that these stereotypes were unfounded. And now, perhaps partly because their findings have filtered down from academia into society at large and partly because the world has changed, these stereotypes have faded. With more research, it's likely that many of the assumptions about gender and personality that live on today will wither and die in the years to come.

ARE BOYS MORE AGGRESSIVE?

The headlines have the staccato rat-a-tat-tat of a gun. A 16-year-old boy in Pearl, Mississippi, killed his mother and then shot nine students at his high school. Two months later, a 14-year-old boy in West Paducah, Kentucky, killed three students and wounded five others at his high school. Three months after that, an 11-year-old and a 13-year-old boy opened fire on a middle school in Jonesboro, Arkansas, killing five people and wounding ten others. In the 14 months that followed, a 14-year-old boy was arrested for shooting a science teacher in Edinboro,

Pennsylvania; an 18-year-old boy was arrested for killing a classmate at his high school in Fayetteville, Tennessee; a 15-year-old boy shot more than twenty people at his high school in Springfield, Oregon and then killed his parents; two high school boys planted pipe bombs and stormed their high school in Littleton, Colorado, with guns, killing fifteen people, including themselves; and a 15-year-old boy shot and wounded six classmates at his high school in Conyers, Georgia.

A common denominator in all these tragedies? Boys were known or suspected of committing them. In the past decade, aggravated assault by teenagers has increased 70 percent, and the number of juveniles arrested for murder has increased by half. Most of those who were arrested and convicted were boys.

One of the few gender differences in personality that researchers agree on is that males are more aggressive than females. Yet parents find it hard to reckon these statistics with the innocent baby boy gurgling and smiling in their arms. Is it really his destiny to become a hitter, a biter, a bully, or worse? Is the question not if but when?

Certainly, not all boys are aggressive, and not all girls are so highly evolved that they settle their conflicts with cooperative words. I came home from work one day to see my son, then 3, with bite marks on his forehead. The child who bit him was a girl—a nice girl, his best friend at the time. They were playing at her house and got into an argument. By the baby-sitter's account, David showed his anger by yelling, Nora by biting. A woman told me that as a high school student, she was cornered in the locker room after swim team practice one day by a group of girls who accused her of looking at them the wrong way. There are certainly individual girls who are more primed for a fight than individual boys. But as a group, boys are more physically aggressive, here and in cultures all over the world.

Boys don't start out this way. In the early years of life, they're no more likely to hit, kick, or assert themselves physically than are girls. The difference in aggressiveness begins to show up at about age 3. It's no coincidence that this is also the time when children start to play *with* other children, instead of simply playing separately, side by side. So it becomes more apparent who has the social graces. When a boy wants a toy that another child has, he's more likely than a girl to rip it out of the child's hands. When a boy is angry or frustrated, he's more apt than a girl to hit someone nearby, be it a classmate, a teacher, a parent, or a sibling. Squabbles between siblings are the most common form of aggression at home. And though sisters and sisters as well as sisters and brothers certainly go at each other with fists and feet, most of the *physical* sibling rivalry is between brothers.

All this points to something biological that makes boys more aggressive. People joke about "testosterone poisoning," implying that the sex hormone is the culprit, and there seems to be some truth to this thinking. Research has found that boys who are bullies have higher testosterone levels than other boys. And girls with adreno-genital syndrome, or AGS, a condition in which they absorbed abnormally high levels of androgens in the womb, start more fights than their sisters do. One theory is that the relatively high levels of testosterone and other androgens that bathe males before birth shape brain development in a way that primes boys to react aggressively to challenges and threats.

On the other hand, an individual's testosterone level rises and falls depending on the situation. Research shows that testosterone spikes in response to a challenge, whether it is a tennis match or some other competition, or a threatening gesture. The testosterone of male monkeys increases when they fight over a female. So testosterone gets pumped up when individuals need to defend or prove themselves.

But testosterone doesn't entirely explain why some people are more aggressive than others. Parents, teachers, and friends influence a child's notions of what kinds of aggressive acts are appropriate, when, and for whom. Parents, especially fathers, roughhouse more with their sons, so boys are more comfortable with playful wrestling and pummeling, the kinds of activities that sometimes escalate into physical fights.

More important, a certain amount of aggressive behavior is considered normal in boys. You don't have to be a behavioral scientist to know this, but behavioral scientists studying adults' attitudes toward aggressive behavior in children have found that people think that such behavior is more acceptable in boys. So, girls probably try harder to tame their aggressive impulses because they learn at their parents' knees that little girls don't hit. One study followed a group of young boys and girls to see if the ones who started out especially aggressive remained that way. The boys who were the most aggressive at age 2 were also the most aggressive at age 5, but the correlation was weaker for girls. It could be that boys are less likely to "outgrow" aggressiveness as they mature because aggressiveness is a more fundamental personality trait for them. But they also have less incentive to try to become less aggressive.

Boys not only learn that it's more acceptable for them to hit, they learn what might be called aggression etiquette: whom and when to hit. Look at a group of preschoolers on the playground. If a boy is hitting a classmate, chances are that it's another boy. It's not hard to see why. Hitting a girl is taboo. And you'll see fewer boys going up and punching other children unprovoked than hitting in self-defense. One reason undoubtedly is that parents tell boys that they shouldn't start fights, but that they should "stand up for their rights." Eleanor Maccoby cited research indicating that even fathers who consider aggressive behavior to be bad for boys are concerned about their sons seeming like "sissies" and thus, however reluctantly, give them the nod to fight back.

Another, probably stronger factor is the attitude of peers. Many children who go around hitting other children are labeled "bullies" and are disliked. The one boy in my son's preschool class who had a reputation for being a bully was also the child who was invited to the fewest birthday parties. This particular bully eventually changed his ways in elementary school, but those who don't are often shunted to the margins of schoolchildren's society. Classmates also tend to reinforce the double standard that parents teach: that aggressive behavior is more acceptable for boys than for girls. And if you factor out children who are shunned as bullies, classmates even find aggressive behavior attractive in boys. One study looked at the popularity of boys and girls in the fourth to sixth grades. It found that boys who fought back were popular, but girls who did so were not. So boys have an incentive to act tough and brawny.

So far, the discussion of aggressive behavior has been confined to physical aggression. But when the definition is broadened to include things like name-calling or snubbing a classmate, then the difference between boys and girls narrows. My daughter was just 2 when she heard a 5-year-old neighbor tell her younger sister, "You're not my friend anymore." These fighting words made such a deep impression on Sarah that she told me over and over again, "Margaret said to Anna, 'You're not my friend anymore.'" I explained that sometimes when kids (Did I say girls?) are angry at each other, they say such things, but that they really don't mean what they say. Soon after, when Sarah and her brother, David, were fighting, Sarah unleashed Margaret's words on him.

Researchers have a name for the You're-not-my-friend-anymore kind of barbs: relational aggression. Only recently have researchers begun studying it, and they're finding that it's every bit as psychologically and socially harmful as beating someone up or threatening to do so. Both kinds of aggression lead to loneliness, depression, and conduct problems in their victims.

Relational aggression can start as early as preschool, and it becomes increasingly common through middle school. And it's not just a phenomenon among American girls. Girls in other cultures use it, too. With the social pressure not to hit, girls have to find more acceptable ways to vent their anger or contempt for the peers they dislike. It stands to reason that girls would fight with words, since they tend to use words well. And they quickly learn that using words specifically to alienate a girl from other girls is one of the worst things they can do to her. Recent research shows that relational aggression is more distressful for girls than for boys, since girls' social lives are built around intimate knots of close friends.

But even when relational aggression is taken into account, boys are still more aggressive than girls. Recent studies of bullying, which encompass both physical and relational aggression, find that boys bully and are bullied more often than girls. For example, a 1999 survey of 3,918 Australian children asked them whether they'd been teased, hit, or bullied in some other way in recent months. Among the 6 year olds who were interviewed, about 26 percent of the boys and 19 percent of the girls had bullied another child and been bullied. Among the 8 year olds, the figures were 30 percent and 19 percent, respectively. And among the 10 year olds, they were 21 percent and 12 percent.

So, a combination of sex hormones and social expectations makes boys more aggressive than girls. But what makes individual boys and girls more aggressive than others? What transforms a sweet baby into a cruel child? The biggest factor is personal exposure to violence, such as being hit or otherwise abused and seeing parents or other people fight viciously. Experiences like these were by far the leading contributors of violent behavior among boys and girls aged 7 to 15 in a 1999 study by researchers at Case Western Reserve University. Second was the failure of parents to control their children by keeping tabs on their whereabouts and setting household rules and enforcing them.

Like earlier research, the Case Western study showed that violent TV shows, movies, and video games were also associated with violent behavior in children. It's not hard to see why. When children see characters triumph by hitting or insulting other people, they come to think that these are acceptable ways to handle conflict, according to the National Association for the Education of Young Children, a professional organization in Washington, D.C. And they may lose some empathy for others, the association's literature says, because watching violent acts makes children see other people as "enemies," rather than as thinking, feeling individuals like themselves. The association suggests that there may be a snowball effect: Children who lack empathy probably are not well liked by peers, and feeling friendless may make them all the more callous and aggressive.

ARE GIRLS MORE NURTURING?

When my daughter was an infant and I'd take her to my son's preschool class, I'd be surrounded in no time by 3 year olds eager to get a peek at the baby. All were girls. When my neighbor brought her newborn daughter to her son's class, she, too, was encircled, but the curious onlookers were equal numbers of boys and girls. Two classes, two different reactions by the boys.

Was one group more typical of boys' interest in babies and, as such, a sign of difference (or similarity) in boys' and girls' nurturing instincts?

These two experiences certainly don't prove or disprove the widely held view that girls are more nurturing than boys, which is to say that girls are more interested in infants and others who are smaller and weaker than they are. But the experiences do illustrate the problem that researchers (and the rest of us) have in settling the issue. Sure, there's evidence of some "maternal instinct" in girls everywhere we look. Girls like to play with dolls more than boys do. But do they like to do so because they are natural-born nurturers and want to practice being mommies or because they're given dolls and encouraged to play with them? In cultures around the world, females do more of the child care. But is this division of labor the result of nature or of sex discrimination that excludes females from other activities? The females of most animal species also raise the young. But animals do a lot of things that we don't do.

One way that scientists try to gauge how nurturing children are is to put them in a room with an infant and see how they react. When one such study was done with 3 year olds, the boys came over and looked at the baby as often as the girls did. But when the study was repeated with 5 year olds, more girls showed an interest in the baby. It's possible that as the boys got older, more of them considered babies (like dolls) to be girls' stuff. But bowing to social pressure to avoid girls' stuff doesn't mean that boys are fundamentally less nurturing than girls.

In another experiment, this one with children aged 8 to 14, the nurturing responses were somewhat mixed. The girls did pay more attention to a baby sitting in a playpen, but when the researchers later measured the children's heart rates and other physiological indicators of arousal as they listened to a record-

47

ing of an infant crying, the girls and boys were equally aroused. In other words, the boys seemed just as concerned about the baby. In the late 1970s, when the study was done, the researchers interpreted the findings to mean that males and females have an equal capacity for nurturing (because their biological responses were equally strong), but that females act more nurturing because society expects them to do so.

Now, many behavioral scientists say that it's just as likely that the reason why girls spend more time cooing at and caring for babies is that they really are more nurturing by nature. As with several other male-female differences, nurturing appears to be related to differences in sex hormone levels. Recall that females are exposed to lower levels of androgens in the womb than males are and that variations in androgens are associated with many things: slight differences in brain structure; more physically aggressive behavior in males; and, the thinking goes, the impulse to nurture.

Some evidence comes from observations of girls born AGS, the disorder caused by exposure to excessive levels of androgens before birth. As preschoolers and schoolgirls, they show less interest in infants than do other girls, and they are indifferent and sometimes downright hostile toward dolls. Estrogen levels are also important. In experiments at the Yerkes Regional Primate Research Center at Emory University in Atlanta, female monkey and chimpanzee fetuses that were injected with estradiol, a form of estrogen, went on to become dramatically more nurturing than other females after birth.

But tracing nurturing behavior exclusively to female biology has proved to be as bedeviling as comparing the numbers of boys and girls who cluster around an infant who is visiting their classroom. The latest turn of the screw comes from the discovery of a gene that promotes maternal behavior in mice.

Although female mice are responsible for nurturing the young, their maternal instinct depends on a gene that they inherit from their fathers. They inherit a copy of the gene from both parents, but the one from the mother is inactive. Male mice who are genetically engineered not to have this gene father female offspring who became such neglectful mothers that their babies die. This gene is active in the hypothalamus and amygdala, regions of the brain that are thought to be involved in reproductive behavior. Just because a genetic source of nurturing behavior in mice comes from the father doesn't mean that the same is true of humans. But humans do have the same nurturing gene found in mice, and its effect on our personalities is waiting to be discovered.

Even if girls are more nurturing than boys in play and in social science experiments, the difference probably doesn't mean a whole lot in the real world. The desire to nurture seems to depend as much on opportunity as it does on biology. When men and boys have to care for a baby or a young child, they do just fine. Research shows that fathers are able to get their infants to take as much milk from a bottle and calm them down just as well as mothers can.

Interest in infants is just one measure of nurturing behavior. Another is interest in a pet. If a puppy, rather than an infant, were put in a playpen in a classroom, chances are there'd be no difference in the number of boys and girls who'd come over to "oo" and "ah." In our house, my son and daughter regularly fight over who gets to feed our cat.

It may well be that different situations bring out the nurturing instinct in boys than in girls. At his birthday party, Eric, a 9 year old who is known and admired for his superior athletic abilities, could see that one of his friends, a less gifted athlete, was struggling to make a basket during a basketball game. Eric empathized with the other boy and took time from the basket-ball game to coach him. Eric's approach wasn't that of a know-it-all, but of a mentor nurturing some much-coveted sports skills in a friend. Research shows that boys and girls are equally empathic and willing to help someone in need. If a classmate is crying, for example, a boy is just as likely as a girl to help or comfort the child. Feeling and sacrificing for others is what nur-turing is all about.

The bottom line is that biology may predispose females to be more nurturing in certain ways, but life experiences, like feeding an infant or raising a puppy or even, perhaps, mentoring a friend, can outweigh biology and bring out the nurturing impulse in anyone, male or female. Researchers think that boys, and society as a whole, stand to benefit if parents give their sons as many of these kinds of opportunities as possible because the more nurturing boys are, the less prone they are to acts of aggression. Carol Nagy Jacklin put it this way: "Nurturing may be an antidote for violence. Thus, it may be even more impor-tant to encourage nurturing qualities in boys than in girls, given the slightly higher average levels of male aggressive behavior."

ARE BOYS MORE ACTIVE?

A colleague at work was describing, with great sympathy, her brother's Saturday morning routine with his two sons aged 1 and 3. The brother and his wife felt compelled to get the boys outdoors so that they could burn off their considerable energy, an activity that they described as "running the dogs." Otherwise, they would pay later, having to endure their children bouncing off the walls in their small house for the rest of the day. My colleague was relieved that her 3-year-old daughter didn't need so much physical activity. Her daughter was content to spend a Saturday morning drawing or sitting on the floor in her room grouping her Playmobile people as she made up stories about them.

As infants, boys and girls are equally active—they spend as much time kicking, waving their arms, arching their backs, rolling over, crawling, and cruising. But after about their first birthday, boys, on average, begin to spend more time on the move, and from then on the gender difference in activity level increases. To be sure, there is tremendous variation from one child to another. There are individual boys who are less active than most girls, and high-energy girls who are more active than most boys. And if you consider "active" in its broadest sense to mean *doing* things—drawing, playing board games, or playing the piano, as opposed to just sitting around watching TV—then there's probably no difference between boys and girls as groups. But this discussion is about *physical* activities, like playing ball; climbing a jungle gym; running; and, at its most basic, moving around. Most studies show that boys are more physically active.

There's no doubt that boys are raised to be more active. Researchers have observed that parents (especially fathers) are more active with sons than with daughters from the time the boys are infants. Parents spend more time doing things like moving their sons' arms and legs as they lie on their backs, jiggling them, holding them football style, and gliding them across the room like submarines. As they get older, boys also have more opportunities for physical activity, with more organized sports available to them.

Although girls have more sports teams now than a generation ago and more parents encourage their daughters to play competitive sports, the gap is far from closed. After elementary school, more girls than boys drop out of organized sports, and girls get less exercise in general. The federal government's 1990 Youth Risk Behavior Survey found that just 25 percent of the high school girls participated in vigorous physical activity three or more days a week, compared with 50 percent of the boys. According to Girls Inc., an advocacy group, many girls stop playing sports for social reasons, like concern that they won't be attractive to boys or that they won't look good in their uniforms. But sports are just part of the picture. Even when they're not playing soccer or baseball, boys spend more time moving around.

As with other differences between boys and girls, your child's activity level may be a function of the level of sex hormones he or she was exposed to before birth and their effect on the brain. High levels of androgens in utero are associated with high activity in the years ahead, but high levels of estrogen and progesterone seem to be linked to relatively low activity. It's possible that different levels of these sex hormones somehow prime the brain to prefer high-energy or quieter play. Girls with AGS, who were exposed to large amounts of androgens before birth, are more active than other girls.

Boys' higher activity level may help explain boys' faster metabolism, the rate at which their bodies burn food energy. Metabolism increases in both boys and girls from birth until age 2, but the increase is sharper in boys. At around age 2, girls' metabolisms slow down, but boys' keep speeding up for another year at least. Maccoby thinks that boys burn energy faster than girls because they move more often or more vigorously.

Scientists have all sorts of ways of measuring activity levels in children. Sometimes they literally count the number of times a boy and a girl move from one place or another or the number of times they move vigorously. Sometimes, they even wire children up with machines that record every arm or leg movement

in a given period. The studies have found that the gender difference can be large or small, depending on the circumstance.

The gender difference tends to be negligible when boys and
girls are playing outside. Preschoolers and elementary school students run, play ball, swing on swings, climb on jungle gyms, and
engage in other gross motor play. Boys and girls don't necessarily
enjoy the same activities and some individual boys and girls exert
more energy than others, but, on the whole, groups of boys and
girls both move around a fair amount. The biggest difference in
activity level can be seen when boys and girls come indoors. Girls
slow down their pace. In the classroom, preschool girls may draw,
play dress-up, or observe the classroom hamster. As elementary
school students, they may sit at their desks and talk to friends until
the teacher tells them to be quiet. But when boys come indoors,
they're still revved up. Preschool boys may ram trucks together,
knock down block towers, or run and jump around the classroom.
After a year or so in elementary school, boys have more self-control, but many still swing their arms or pummel each other as they
walk down the halls and kick the legs of their desks before they
finally settle down to focus on schoolwork.

Maccoby and others have found that whether they're
indoors or outdoors, boys are most active when they're with
other boys. Certainly, parents and other caregivers can attest to
the fact that when boys play together, the energy level increases.
Boys often run around outside (or inside), and even if they're
engaged in a quiet activity like playing a computer game,
chances are that they're not quiet; they shift in their chairs or
dance around the computer table. Girls become louder and
more active when a friend comes over, too, but Maccoby says
that the increase in activity level is not as great as it is for boys.

What happens when a boy and a girl play together? Does
the girl make the boy less active, or does the boy make the girl

more active? Researchers don't know because they haven't studied the questions. But I know that when my daughter has a play date with a boy after school, they're rarely wild. She and the boy sometimes look at books, do puzzles, play computer games, or play on the backyard swings. If anything, Sarah's wilder when she's playing with another girl. It could be that children are more active with the children they're most comfortable with. Researchers say that from preschool until adolescence, most children are most comfortable with playmates of their own sex because they're the ones with whom they spend the most time.

Of course, even extremely active boys are not perpetual motion machines. They slow down when they're alone. Research has found that when boys are alone, they are almost as quiet as girls. They sit still and do a puzzle or play a video game or do something similarly subdued, depending on their interests. But even when they're "quiet," they're moving. "They do show more restless, squirmy movements when staying in one place," notes Carol Nagy Jacklin.

I'll say. When my son tells me about his day in school, he rarely stands still. He's apt to be winding up like a baseball pitcher or sliding across the kitchen floor to an imaginary home plate. When he's watching a ball game alone, he bounces on the chair like a rodeo rider (that is, when he's not dashing off the chair to slide into home). I don't know of any girls who relax so actively.

ARE GIRLS MORE SOCIAL?

The mother of a girl and the father of a boy in the same preschool class were comparing their children's social lives. Rachel has started having sleepovers. She has a few close girlfriends in the class, including Melissa, an especially pretty girl and a stylish dresser whom the other girls admire. The mother was concerned because her daughter's mood rose or fell, depending on whether Melissa was nice to her or not that day.

Jack's social life was far simpler. The boy had friends in the class, but never mentioned or seemed bothered if one wasn't nice to him. What counted to him were the activities that they did together, like riding bikes or building with Legos. The father was also surprised to hear that 4-year-old girls were having sleepovers already. Jack, his friends, and his friends' parents never even mentioned the word.

The conversation ended with the two parents agreeing that it's easier being a boy because the social machinations that girls struggle to master are over their heads.

If you consider "social" to mean forming intimate friendships, then girls are more social than boys. As early as preschool, but certainly by the lower grades of elementary school, many girls have a "best friend" in whom they confide their deep feelings and evolving opinions. Perhaps girls are able to make close friends because of their keen skill in reading people's emotions, as conveyed by facial expressions, body language, and changes in tone of voice. Studies in which children listened to short stories and then answered questions about the characters' feelings suggest that girls as young as 3 have better social intuition than do boys.

There may even be a genetic basis for this sort of skill. British researchers recently traced social acumen to the X chromosome inherited from the father. The finding was based on a small study of girls with Turner's syndrome, a disorder characterized by normal intelligence but often social adjustment problems in which one or both the X chromosomes is broken or missing. Girls with a single X chromosome inherited from their fathers were significantly better adjusted socially than girls with a single X from their mothers. If some degree of social skill really does arise from the paternal X chromosome, then it stands to reason that boys would be less adept socially than girls, since they inherit their only X chromosome from their mothers. No one is saying that a person's social intelligence is all in his or her genes, rather that it's the product of that person's experience pushing and pulling against a genetic predisposition.

Whatever the reason, boys as a rule don't know their friends nearly as well as girls do. They don't talk much about their feelings, unless it's to say something about which foods, movies, or toys they like or dislike. When they talk about themselves it's often to boast about something "amazing" that they did, like being the first one done with a test or hitting a home run. Otherwise, they discuss mainly impersonal things, like what they're going to do and the rules of whatever game they're playing. Among school-age boys, of course, sports is a perennial topic: the Yankees' lineup, so-and-so's batting average, the theoretical minimum number of pitches that can be thrown in a game (given that a game has to go just four and a half innings to be counted).

But being "social" means more than being close and confessional with a best friend. When seen in the broadest terms of wanting to be with others and figuring out how to fit in, boys are every bit as social as girls. Infant boys and girls seem equally social in the sense that they show more interest in faces than in inanimate objects. But baby boys and baby girls show their social needs in different ways. Infant girls make eye contact with people longer than infant boys do, but infant boys seem to have an even greater desire for their parents' attention, which they show by crying more and for longer periods when they are upset. As preschoolers and older children, boys are no more likely than girls to stand alone on the playground (although there are always some boys and girls who do).

The size and dynamics of boys' and girls' groups are also different. For one thing, boys tend to play in larger groups than do girls. Another difference is that girls try harder to avoid offending a friend. If two girls disagree on what to do, they'll try to compromise. Studies show that if several children want to do something, girls are better than boys are at taking turns. If a girl's effort at cooperation fails, she's less likely to confront another girl directly than to tell the parent or other caregiver on hand and let the adult talk to the girl.

It's not that girls are basically nicer than boys. They cooperate because cooperation works for them socially. Since girls tend to play in pairs or in small groups, they have a lot to lose by offending even just one friend. Getting too bossy or appearing mean can cost a girl her social life, at least temporarily. Indeed, when girls are being nasty, they'll go to great lengths to hide it. Carol Beal, of the University of Massachusetts in Amherst, notes that one strategy used by girls of elementary-school age and older who are angry with a girl is to pass along criticism about her to one another without identifying themselves as the critics ("I heard she did X, and it's really bad to do that because . . . ").

In one respect, boys are more social than girls: They are more easily swayed by other boys than girls are by other girls. This finding may come as a surprise to someone who sees girls wearing similar clothes and hairstyles. To be sure, from about age 2 on, both girls and boys are influenced by their friends and do what they feel it takes to win their approval. But here's the difference. Given the choice of pleasing the teacher (or a parent) or a group of same-sex peers, boys are more inclined than girls to play to the crowd. Boys as young as 2 are more responsive to other boys than to teachers at preschool or day care, whereas girls are equally responsive to both. Boys' tendency to follow other boys grows stronger in elementary school. If a boy does something that makes the other boys laugh, he'll keep doing it, even if the teacher tells him to stop. Any wonder why the class clown is usually a boy?

Child development experts think that boys are more intensely focused on one another than on adults because they're trying to separate themselves from females. After all, in the early years, the adults who spend the most time with them are women: their mothers, their nannies, child care workers in day care, and preschool teachers. So, boys look to other boys for clues on how to behave like a boy. Imitating a boy is a surefire way to get it right. Part of the process of separating from adults—especially women—is misbehaving or, at least, testing limits. Many researchers who study boys think that the thrill of doing things like being cutups in class helps boys bond with one another.

ARE BOYS MORE POWER HUNGRY?

One of the biggest differences between boys and girls is that boys are more intent on dominating others. Boys' friendships are based, to a large extent, on one-upsmanship—one boy try- ing to prove to others that he's stronger, faster, smarter, you name it. The jousting for power begins in nursery school and intensifies in elementary school. Of course, any playground has its alpha males and alpha females, so boys aren't the only ones who are into power. But it's a bigger issue for boys. "The ques- tion of who is tougher than whom seems to be much more salient to boys than to girls, and more efforts to establish or maintain dominance may be seen among boys than among girls," Maccoby wrote in *The Two Sexes*.

Researchers who have observed preschoolers and elemen- tary school students say that boys try to establish their dominance as soon as they meet a new group of boys. A preschool boy may do so by snatching a toy from another boy to see what he does. If the second boy can't manage to get the toy back, the first one is dominant. In elementary school, a boy may prove his dominance by excelling in sports or arguing louder or more forcefully than the others about the rules of a game. Studies show that dominance hierarchies form more quickly and remain more stable as boys get older. So, it's clearer who's boss in the third grade than in kindergarten.

What it means for a boy to be the dominant one in a group is that other boys don't act aggressively toward him or challenge him in other ways. They, in turn, try to assert themselves over other boys—often those who are new to the group—by pushing them around and seeing how well they fight back. A boy who challenges a more dominant boy is taking a risk. The dominant boy may hit him and hurt him. Or he may humiliate him, for example, by showing that he's better at dunking a basketball or doing something else that's considered cool.

When the third-grade boys play kickball during recess at my son's school, the best players run the show. They decide who kicks first and who gets the most turns. Some of these boys cheat by insisting on kicking every time their team is up, even though that means that several other boys don't get any turns. Most of the other boys don't challenge this brazen flouting of the rules, and those who do are usually ignored. Some storm off in frustration, but those who want to remain in the game are forced to go along. Boys survive in a group by knowing their place in it. And the incentive for boys at the bottom of the dominance hierarchy to stay in the group is that there's strength in numbers. In other words, being part of a group makes them feel powerful.

Boys can't always be in a group, of course—a whole baseball team can't come over for a play date. Outside school, boys might play with one or two friends at a time. But even then, they're often trying to outdo each other. Their attempts to dominate are not necessarily aggressive or even hostile. They can be good-natured put-downs like the one my son kept shouting at his friend Jeffrey when they were playing catch one afternoon. Whenever Jeffrey missed the ball, David would shout, "Error!" Jeffrey dished the criticism right back when David missed a catch.

In general, girls don't have as great a need as boys to dominate their friends. If anything, their desire to cooperate and be "nice" makes them bend over backward to be fair and equitable. Campbell Leaper, a psychologist at the University of California at Santa Cruz, notes that when a girl wants to do something, she'll state her preference as a suggestion, as in "Let's do . . ." Boys, on the other hand, tend to give orders like, "Give me that." In such exchanges, the dominant boy barks the command and the subordinate boy usually complies.

Every school has its alpha girls—popular girls who, because of their popularity, are dominant. But even they tend not to use the confrontational style of alpha boys to assert their superiority. They're cagier, as shown by a study in which a group of four boys and a group of four girls had to take turns watching a movie. The movie was threaded through a projector that had been designed so that several people could operate it but only one could watch the movie at a time. In each group, a leader emerged who got the others to do most of the work. The dominant boy shoved the other boys away and used other physically intimidating tactics. The dominant girl got her way by sweet-talking the other girls into believing that she needed to see the movie more than they did.

Of course, girls can be quite bossy at times. Who hasn't known someone like Angelica, the domineering girl in *Rugrats*, the popular cartoon TV show about young children? But bossy girls learn by trial and error how far they can go and with whom. A girl will continue to push around a girl who doesn't complain about it or who wants her friendship badly enough. Or, like Angelica, a girl will boss around younger children. But unlike a bossy boy, who's seen as tough and strong, a bossy girl is regarded as, well, too bossy. Angelica will never win a popularity contest.

Girls who are too bossy often learn the hard way to change their ways with friends. I used to cringe when I'd hear my daughter, at age 4, pushing around play dates by saying things like, "It's my house, so I get to pick which game we play." None of the girls challenged her (maybe they were trying to cooperate). But as she got closer to 5, I noticed her softening her tone. If she and a girl-friend wanted to do different things, they'd try to accommodate each other, saying things like, "OK, first we'll draw, then we'll dress up like lions," or "You can draw here, and I'll build with Lincoln Logs on the floor there." Sarah and her friends were learning that they had to cooperate in order to stay friends.

Jackie, a first grader, suffered the consequences of being too domineering. She kept trying to control Robin by ordering her to stop playing with a third girl in their class. Jackie would say, "If you play with her, I won't be your friend." Instead, Robin stopped playing with Jackie, and gradually so did several other girls in the class.

ARE GIRLS MORE FEARFUL?

The nursery rhyme about Little Miss Muffet being frightened by the spider introduced us to and reinforced the idea that girls are easily scared. Images of squeamish little girls running away from spiders and snakes seem quaint today at a time of courageous female characters like Mulan and Buffy the Vampire Slayer. But even as girls flaunt the voguish "Girl Power" slogan, psychological surveys find that they still scare more easily than boys.

Most of the studies found in an electronic search of the scientific literature on fearfulness and gender reached the conclusion that girls are more fearful. It was even the same when children rated how fearful they thought other children were. Boys and girls alike rated girls as being more fearful than boys.

Why? Are girls more fearful by nature, or are they made that way by a society that allows and expects them to be scared? Is fearfulness the legacy of all the years of females being unequal to males? Is Little Miss Muffet a greater influence on girls than is Mulan?

First, a word about the possible shortcomings of the psychological studies on gender differences in fearfulness. Some of the studies are based on reports of parents or teachers, so they may be colored by gender bias. And while some of the surveys are of children assessing themselves, it could be that boys are less willing to admit to fears because they think that they're expected to be courageous. So girls may not have more, or more intense, fears; they may just be more honest about them.

I asked my son about his third-grade classmates: Are boys and girls equally fearful, or does one group scare more easily?

"Girls are more scared," he said.

"Why?"

"They just are."

"Why? Give me an example."

He had to think for a while. Then he said, "In gym when we play tag, if we run up and try to tag a girl, most of the girls will run away and go, 'Aahhh,' instead of trying to tag us."

Afterward, he proceeded to list all the girls who were exceptions. I said, "If there are so many girls who don't run away, why do you think girls are more easily scared?"

"Because girls are *supposed* to be more scared."

"What do you mean?"

"You know," he said. "Boys are supposed to be tough."

"Does that mean boys and girls are equally scared, but boys try to hide it so that they can look tough?"

He looked away and changed the subject. I'd hit a nerve.

Of course, boys get scared. Studies show that in general they're afraid of many of the same things as girls: getting hurt, getting in trouble, dying, or having a loved one die. And when girls are found to scare more easily and intensely, the difference is slight. When Disney released *The Lion King*, there were numerous newspaper articles about how frightening it was, especially the scene in which King Mufasa was graphically forced to his death by his evil brother, Scar. Many child development experts debated whether such material was too scary for preschoolers. But no one said that it was too scary only for girls.

In some households, it's the boys who scare more easily than their sisters. When my friend Susan took her twin 4 year olds to a Halloween party, Chloe went through the dark, spooky room all by herself and Nicholas would only go in holding his mother's hand. Based on this and other experiences, Susan was convinced that, at least during this period of their lives, Nicholas was more fearful than Chloe. At times, I've had the same impression of my children. When a storm knocked the electricity out of our house, my son, then 7, panicked. He cried, stayed close to us, and slept with two flashlights in his bed. His 3 1/2-year-old sister remained calm.

It's difficult for parents to assess the relative fearfulness of their sons and daughters, unless the children are twins because age makes a big difference. As children get older, they become less fearful of monsters and other supernatural phenomena and more fearful of real-life threats like dangerous situations or failure. And boys and girls fear different things. In a 1999 study of 8- to 12 year olds, Nancy Ryan-Wenger, of Ohio State University, found that more of the girls were afraid of natural occurrences like thunder and lightning, whereas more of the boys cited intruders with guns and scary amusement park rides. The boys also reported being more frightened of getting into trouble and failing in school, which is understandable since boys do face more discipline and academic problems. (For more information, see Chapter 4, pages 177–80.)

Jerome Kagan, a professor of psychology at Harvard, makes perhaps the strongest case for girls being more fearful overall. His evidence is a long-term study that used objective measures, such as heart rate, brain activity, and controlled scientific observations of children in frightening situations. Some examples were having electrodes placed on their chests, having an adult speak sternly to them, or looking up from play and being surprised by a clown entering the room. From the time they were toddlers, the girls showed more fear.

The first clues to a fearful disposition were seen when the children were infants. Most of the children—both boys and girls—who turned out to be fearful had been "high reactive" 4 month olds, meaning that they had strong reactions to new stimuli, such as the sharp smell of rubbing alcohol and the sight of a bright, new mobile. They cried; fussed; kicked their legs; flailed their arms; and, in general, moved around a lot. Most of the children who turned out not to be especially fearful had been "low reactive" infants—the opposite of the high reactives. So reactivity was interpreted as a precursor of fearfulness.

At 4 months, the infant boys and girls were about equally reactive. But at 14 months old, slightly more girls showed fear in the experiments, regardless of how reactive they'd been earlier, and the gender difference increased as the children grew. Not only did most of the girls (as well as boys) who were fearful at 14 months remain that way, but a significant proportion of the girls—15 percent—who showed little fear at 14 months became extremely fearful later on. In contrast, just 6 percent of the boys who seemed relatively fearless at 14 months became fearful.

From 2 years old until 13, the girls were more inhibited, a trait associated with fearfulness. And of the boys and girls who were initially considered to be inhibited, a greater share of the girls stayed that way. To cite but two examples: They took longer to talk to a child or an adult they did not know and avoided taking risks when playing a game that was set up to test their appetite for risk taking. A test for 5 year olds was to throw a ball into a basket. The children could stand as close or as far away as they wanted to. The inhibited children stood about two feet away. The uninhibited children stood as much as five feet away, and it seemed to Kagan that they relished the challenge. The inhibited children were characterized as more fearful, in general, by their mothers than were the uninhibited children.

Of course, all the children were afraid of something during the years of testing. But a small group was intimidated by very few of the challenges thrown their way. "Some behaved as if nothing short of serious physical harm could frighten them," Kagan wrote in his book, *Galen's Prophecy*. All were boys.

The fearful and inhibited children were physiologically different in several ways from the fearless and uninhibited children. They tended to have higher heart rates in challenging circumstances and higher levels of cortisol and other stress hormones in their blood. Their facial muscles tended to tense up and their pupils to dilate, signs of activity in the amygdala, a part of the brain that is involved in emotioal response and considered the likely origin of fear. And the brains of fearful, inhibited children were more active in the right frontal region than in the left. The right frontal region is associated with emotional distress. Adults who are shy, anxious, or depressed show more activation in this region than do people who are extroverts and neither anxious nor depressed.

There's strong evidence that a gene or genes influence whether a child is inhibited or uninhibited. Although a "fearfulness gene" has yet to be found, Kagan thinks that there's a good chance that it's sex linked, meaning that more girls than boys may inherit it. Kagan also thinks that differences in the brain partially explain why girls are slightly more fearful. Since androgens, the "male" hormones, influence nerve cells in the amygdala, it's plausible that they may be responsible for gender differences in this probable fear center.

All this sounds as though girls are naturally fearful and there's not much parents and others can do about it. But that's not the case. The biological underpinnings of fearfulness amount to a tendency, not fate. Kagan thinks that the reason for the sharp rise in fearfulness in girls during the second year of life is that they learn to be afraid by well-meaning parents and caregivers who hover a bit too closely or give too many warnings to be careful. Studies show that parents tend to overprotect their daughters more than their sons. But Kagan's research has found that children who are allowed to look run-of-the-mill childhood fears in the face—continuing to play on the playground after they fall down, for example—are less likely to grow fearful than children who are coddled, regardless of their temperaments as infants.

ARE BOYS MORE COMPETITIVE?

Finding examples of competitiveness among boys is as easy as collecting shells on the beach: They're so numerous, you can pick your favorites. Watch elementary school children on the playground during recess, and you're likely to see groups of mainly boys playing soccer, kickball, or some other competitive sport and groups of mainly girls talking, climbing on the monkey bars, or doing something else that's not as competitive. This isn't to say that *all* the boys are playing ball or that *no* girls are. And it's quite possible that what looks from a distance like a friendly conversation among girls is really a showdown over who's *in* and who's *out*. But competitive behavior is more obvious in boys.

Girls are every bit as competitive as boys in competitive situations. By most accounts, girls and boys are just as driven to get good grades and win spelling bees and achieve honors at school. Girls on sports teams certainly play to win. Kim, the mother of a girl and a boy in Santa Cruz, California, recalled the "competitive friction" of the girls at her daughter's eighth birthday party, which included a series of swimming contests in their backyard pool. "Most of the girls were so determined to win, they made up excuses if they lost," she said. "Some even persisted and tried to talk me out of giving the winners their prizes!"

Still, from watching and listening to groups of boys and girls, you can't help but get the sense that they're competitive in different ways. Some researchers say that girls are more inclined to compete by measuring themselves against an absolute standard, like the correct form for doing the backstroke or the guidelines for doing a book report, whereas boys like to compete just for the hell of it. Barrie Thorne, a sociologist at the University of California, Berkeley, notes that boys don't just compete when there's competition; they turn ordinary activities into contests. In her book, *Gender Play*, she described watching some elementary school boys climbing on a dirt pile on the school playing field. First, they compared the gripping power of their shoes on the dirt pile. Then they had a "falling contest" to see who could fall the farthest.

Twelve-year-old Janna thinks that boys have a harder time when they lose a competition. Speaking of the coed sports teams at her elementary school in Connecticut, she said that the girls and boys were all driven to win, but that if they lost, some of the boys would get so worked up over a defeat that they'd cry. None of the girls did.

On the basis of her years of observing children, Eleanor Maccoby says that boys are more aroused by competition. She describes competitiveness as one of the "most distinctive male patterns." It's not just that boys spend more time playing sports on the playground during recess or watching football on TV on Sunday afternoon. They spend more time talking about competition. Listen to school-aged boys talk and count how many times they use words like *best, worst, won, lost, most, least, first* and *last*. Boys are often (some parents may think *always*) keeping score.

Research has found that boys as young as 4 pay more attention to competitive activities and dwell more on winning and losing than girls do. Boys show more interest in sports, are more apt to challenge one another by saying things like, "Bet you can't do this" or "Watch me do this," and do more pretend fighting. In one study in which 10- to 12-year-old boys and girls were observed in groups, boys spent half their time in competitive activities and girls spent just 1 percent of their time this way.

Traditional computer games like *Rodent's Revenge*, whose kill-or-be-killed formats are brazenly competitive, appeal mainly to boys. Software companies know this, so when they wanted to tap the female market, they developed noncompetitive activities based on things like writing stories, making movies, or designing clothes. The bestselling girl's software is *Barbie's Fashion Designer*, which enables girls to dress Barbie on the computer with clothes that they create. Even in cultures where there is no *Rodent's Revenge* or *Barbie's Fashion Designer*, researchers say that competition plays a bigger role in boys' lives. Boys find other competitive games to play.

What makes boys more openly competitive? Testosterone is related to a competitive spirit. It rises just before people—males and females—begin any form of competition. High levels of testosterone in the womb may shape males' brains in a way that primes boys to thrill more than do girls to the prospect of competition, much as it appears to prime them to more behave more aggressively.

But researchers have focused mainly on social factors that bring out competitiveness in boys. One theory is that boys start out more comfortable with competition because their parents roughhouse more with them than with their sisters beginning in infancy. But it doesn't take long for boys to see that competition is central to male behavior, especially (but by no means only) when they watch sports. There's no question that boys like to imitate the largely male sports heroes whose glories they see on TV. But it's a chicken-and-egg situation. Watching sports may ratchet up boys' competitive spirit to some degree, but being competitive may be one reason why boys like to watch sports in the first place.

Boys are most competitive in the company of other boys. Competition between boys isn't usually hostile or aggressive, even though it may seem that way. I remember when my son was in first grade and had a boy in his class over for the first time, the two of them got into a discussion about who was in the top reading group. This boy said that he was. David said that he was. I thought that if this confrontational style continued, the friendship would go no where. The style continued, and the friendship has endured.

I would have been wrong to do what I was tempted to do after that play date, which is to tell David that it's not nice to brag. Recent research on boys' friendships suggests that the kind of bragging that David and his friend were engaged in wasn't rude, at least not to boys. To the contrary, it was a bonding experience. Psychologists who study boys' behavior, like William Pollack of Harvard, say that friendly competition is how boys build friendships. Whether it's by boasting about their accomplishments, shooting baskets, or standing around the computer as one boy tests his ability to vanquish the enemy, the effect is the same. "Where boys are seeking to feel part of the action and striving for excellence in the company of their buddies, they are building relationships," Pollack wrote in his book, *Real Boys*.

Every female knows that girls can be intensely competitive in social situations. But in contrast to boys, girls' competitiveness is often anything but friendly ("Did you see her hair? Gross!"). A girl who boasts about herself the way my son and his friend did is less likely to win friends than to lose them. It's easy to imagine the gossip: "She thinks she's *better* than everybody else!" (Read: Stay away from her.) Since competition between girls is usually indirect and often mean spirited, it's not surprising that many girls are initially uneasy when they find themselves in situations that demand that they compete against friends. Carole Beal, of the University of Massachusetts, tells the story of a coach of a college women's athletic team who said that her biggest problem was that team members who were close friends did not want to compete against each other in practice drills.

It's not only the presence of girlfriends on the opposite team that can weaken girls' drive to compete; it's the presence of boys. Some research shows that girls give in too easily when competing against boys. As early as preschool, girls are less likely to challenge a boy who takes a toy away from them than they are to challenge a girl. In a study of elementary school children playing dodgeball, girls were just as skilled as boys at throwing the ball, hitting a target, and jumping out of the ball's way so as not to get hit, but they did their best when they played on girls-only teams. When they played against boys, they didn't do as well as they could.

It's tempting to argue that girls are intimidated by boys' greater physical strength. But that doesn't explain why many girls stop raising their hands in class by around the third or fourth grade. The assistant principal at the elementary school in my town says it's because the girls give up trying to compete for attention with the boys, who tend to be louder and quicker to shout out the answers. She says that teachers in the school are aware of this situation and make special efforts to draw girls into class discussions, with a good degree of success. But she also realizes that teachers can't do it all. At home, she tells her daughter that it's important for her to keep raising her hand to answer questions in class to learn as much as possible.

Scientific evidence makes a strong case for competition being a more central feature of boys' personalities. But even if some biological mechanism is driving them to compete, it's impossible to dismiss the influence of nurture. Until relatively recently, competitive endeavors like higher education and organized sports were only for boys. While fathers and coaches were urging boys to get out there and win, mothers were telling girls to stay out of the fray and "be nice."

Although girls are now excelling in the competitive world of education and sports, they may still be distracted at times by an inner voice that tells them to pull back and be nice. But some researchers think that that voice will grow fainter as competition becomes more common—and more socially acceptable—for girls.

ARE GIRLS MORE EMOTIONAL?

One day, 8-year-old Lauren came home from school in tears. "She was sobbing so hard, she couldn't even talk," her mother said. "I had to sit her down at the kitchen table and wait until she calmed down." Lauren said that the bus driver, who was new and known for being testy, drove past her friend Matthew's bus stop. When Matthew asked the driver to turn around, she refused at first. The driver eventually did circle back to Matthew's bus stop, but only after yelling at him for not reminding her where his bus stop was.

A few days later, Lauren's mother called Matthew's mother to discuss the incident. "She didn't know what I was talking about," Lauren's mother said. "Matthew hadn't told her. And he hadn't seemed at all upset."

Maybe Matthew was good at hiding his feelings. But it's also possible that by the time he got home, his unpleasant encounter with the bus driver was, emotionally speaking, history. Lauren, on the other hand, couldn't put the incident behind her so quickly. The different reactions could be chalked up to differences in these particular children's personalities, except that their reactions fit so neatly the stereotypical view that females are more emotional than males.

This stereotype is so widespread that even preschoolers believe it. In studies, children as young as 3 have said that they think women are happier as well as sadder than men. It's true that schoolgirls and women talk more about their feelings and become more easily upset by certain experiences, like having an argument with a friend. It's also true that they dwell more heavily on sadness and other negative feelings. But females are not more emotional than males at all ages and in all respects.

At birth, boys and girls show the same range of emotions,

such as contentment, fear, and anger. But from about 6 months until at about 6 years, boys are the ones who cry, and cry for longer periods, when they're scared, upset, or frustrated. The following situations upset many boys and girls, but they seem to hit boys especially hard: separating from a parent to go to school, not getting as much attention as they want from a parent, and trying to build something and having it repeatedly fall down. No one knows why young boys are more emotional than young girls, but one likely reason is that areas of the brain that are responsible for self-control are slower to develop, notably the frontal lobes. (For more information on self-control, see Chapter 1, pages 27–29.)

Of course, young boys show their emotions in more complex and positive ways than simply being out of control. As any parent of a son knows, boys can be extremely affectionate, running up to greet their mothers, fathers, and grandparents with welcoming hugs and snuggling close for a bedtime story. A number of mothers I know have remarked on how sweet and sensitive their sons are, too sensitive for their own good in a world of superficial relationships and fickle friends. My eyes still well up with tears when I recall the day when I happened to pass my son's first-grade class lined up in the school hallway, and my son was so happy to see me that he shouted, "I love you, Mommy."

Boys don't stay more openly emotional than girls. Other forces come into play that raise girls' emotional awareness and sensitivity in the months and years ahead. During the period when boys are venting more frustration and begging their mothers for one last kiss before bedtime, girls are getting in touch with their feelings and other people's. Mothers talk to their daughters more often about emotions—whether they liked or disliked someone, whether they were scared, surprised, sad, or upset about something. One study measured the amount of time mothers spent talking about emotions to their 18-month-old children. There was one-third more of this sort of talk with daughters than with sons.

As children get older and more verbal, the difference in emotion-talk increases. In one study, researchers counted the number of times mothers talked about feelings with their 2 year olds. The count was 3.3 times per hour with their daughters and 1.6 times with their sons. It isn't just that mothers sit around ruminating on their feelings. They slip emotional references into all sorts of conversations, even when they're disciplining their daughters. Researchers have found that when daughters misbehave, mothers often tell them that they've upset their friend or whoever else is present. With boys, on the other hand, mothers simply tell them to stop. So it is not surprising that by age 2, girls are also initiating more talk about their feelings, especially with their mothers.

It's not just that parents talk more about emotions with their daughters; the content is different. Robyn Fivush, a psychologist at Emory University who studies gender development, has found that mothers talk more about sadness with their 3-year-old daughters and more about anger with their sons that age. For example, when daughters got into squabbles with friends, their mothers would ask if the fight made them feel sad and then discuss ways to smooth things over. With sons, on the other hand, mothers were more inclined to focus on how angry the sons felt. In Fivush's research, the mothers of sons didn't spend as much time exploring ways to resolve the conflict as did the mothers of daughters, but they did sometimes talk about getting even, a subject that did not come up once between the mothers and daughters. In real life, of course, some mothers and daughters do talk about ways to get back at a nasty classmate, but Fivush's study suggests that such talk is less common with daughters than with sons.

Even today, when many parents go to great lengths to coax their sons to express their feelings, researchers find that many other parents and other adults still discourage boys from getting emotional. Boys who cry in public are told, "Don't be a cry-baby!" Eleanor Maccoby raised the possibility that parents have less tolerance for emotional displays by their sons since their sons tend to have more of them in the early years. But, she said, it's also pretty clear that parents are concerned that if their sons get too emotional, they'll seem weak and be easy targets for the bullies lurking on the playground.

How much do these early differences in emotion-talk at home matter in the long run? Not all studies show that the girls whose mothers talked to them the most about feelings became the most emotionally sensitive. But some research does show a connection. Two long-term studies found that children whose parents talked about emotions with them when they were young developed a greater awareness of other people's feelings than did children whose parents avoided such talk.

Still, Fivush and other researchers don't think that the differences in the amount of time parents spend on emotion-talk with sons and daughters entirely explain the differences in the amount of time boys and girls spend focusing on feelings. There's evidence that females are more attuned to emotions by nature. Mothers may talk more about emotions to girls not only because they consider it a more gender-appropriate activity, but because they find girls more interested. Those early conversations with their moms about feelings may amplify an innate tendency in girls to respond to expressions of emotions.

Girls as young as 3 are better than boys at figuring out how a person feels. They know, for example, that just because a person looks happy doesn't mean that he or she is happy. In the most comprehensive study on emotional intelligence, children aged 3 to 5 listened to stories in which a character had reason to hide his or her emotions. One story involved a sister who wanted to get back at her brother for doing something nasty to her. The sister then hid her brother's favorite toy. When the brother came home and couldn't find his toy, the sister was happy, but tried not to show it.

The children were asked questions to make sure that they understood the stories. Then they were shown drawings of faces showing happy, sad, and neutral expressions. The children were asked which face best conveyed how the sister really felt when her brother couldn't find his toy and which face conveyed how she was pretending to feel. The girls showed better understanding of the real and apparent emotions.

Perhaps girls' more finely tuned sensitivity to other people's feelings explains why the assistant principal of the elementary school in my town has a harder time helping girls resolve conflicts with their classmates. If two children have an ongoing fight that interferes with their ability to cope in school, they often wind up in her office. "With the boys, you talk about the conflict once, and then they go off and forget about it," she says. "With the girls, you talk about the conflict one day, and they're back the next day, saying things like, 'She gave me a mean look.'"

It really does seem that girls are more interested in emotions and that as a result they have greater emotional intelligence. But that doesn't mean that boys are any less emotional deep down. There's no evidence that boys are any less joyful as they blow out their birthday candles and open their presents or that they are any less grieved when a loved one dies. They just work harder to bury their feelings. Certainly, they're under social pressure to do so, but is social pressure the whole explanation? Or is hiding and even denying their emotions part of a boy's basic nature? That's a question awaiting research.

Fivush says that the different degree of attention that boys and girls pay to emotions has significant implications for their well-being during childhood, adolescence, and beyond. Holding in feelings, as boys tend to do, has been linked to violence, substance abuse, and depression. On the other hand, the habit of dwelling on negative emotions, as girls tend to do, is also associated with depression. So, boys and girls may be better served in the long run if they could be more like each other emotionally, with boys learning to recognize and express their feelings more and girls learning to put feelings, especially bad feelings, behind them.

SUMMING UP

Unlike in storybooks, personality traits don't break down neatly by gender in real life. When researchers look at the relationship between gender and personality, more often than not they fail to find one. Whether a child is a girl or a boy has no bearing on whether that child is optimistic or pessimistic or social or reserved or possesses most other such characteristics.

But there are a few exceptions. Boys are indeed more aggressive than girls. They spend far more time play-fighting, as well as bullying and being bullied. Boys are also more active. Not only do they channel more energy into physical activities like sports, they have more nervous energy, which they burn off by swinging their arms, kicking the air, and jumping around long after they've put the ball away and are supposed to be settling down. In addition, boys are more domineering. They organize themselves into larger, more hierarchical groups than girls do, in which there is a leader—often someone with superior athletic ability— and other members jockeying for the second and third tiers by acting tough or showing off their skills.

Showing off is a bonding experience for boys, one of the main ways that they make friends.

Girls, on the other hand, appear more fearful by nature. In careful, ongoing scientific research, they show more fearfulness than boys, for example, by shying away from taking risks and displaying certain physical reactions to stress, such as increased heart rate.

Like other gender differences in behavior, the ones related to personality don't apply to all boys and girls and therefore may not be true for your son or daughter. These characteristics are tendencies for boys and girls to think, feel, and act in certain ways. Researchers think that there are biological reasons yet to be discovered for these tendencies, but that their expression depends to some degree on social factors. For example, girls become more fearful as they get older, an indication that they're raised to see the world as a scary place. Studies show that parents are more protective of daughters than of sons. Studies also show that children who are overprotected become more fearful than do those who are permitted to fall down and learn from their mistakes.

Other gender differences in personality seem to favor either boys or girls. Researchers do say that boys are more openly competitive and that girls are more openly emotional and nurturing. But researchers stop short of asserting that that these traits really do relate to gender, in part, because they have not been carefully studied but also because, as anyone can see, girls compete hard when the situation demands it and boys can be extremely caring and sensitive. If there is a gender difference in these characteristics, it probably has less to do with temperament than with opportunity. Boys have traditionally had more opportunity and encouragement to compete and girls to nurture, as well as to talk about their feelings.

SUGGESTIONS FOR PARENTS

Your child's personality is a set of traits that define who he or she is. Though these traits are fairly stable, they are amenable to change. Of course, there's no reason to try to change an aspect of your child's personality unless it is potentially harmful to the child or others, as aggression and extreme fearfulness can be. Here are some ways that parents can offset the tendencies for boys to be aggressive and girls to be fearful.

Avoid Coercive Discipline. Coercive discipline can mean spanking, threatening ("If you don't get off the slide this minute, you'll be in trouble."), and barking orders ("Get down from that slide right now!"). Children who are disciplined mainly in these ways become more aggressive over time. Parents may argue that they resort to these techniques because their children are especially difficult to control. But it's the most difficult children who turn the most aggressive under harsh discipline, according to research by Jay Belsky of Penn State University.

Belsky followed a group of boys from infancy until they were 5. The children whose parents were the most coercive became the most aggressive and defiant by age 5, whereas the children whose parents were the least coercive (They said things like, "Let's go home now," instead of, "Get off the slide this minute, or else!") became the least aggressive. Here's the most interesting part: The relationship between the style of discipline and aggressive behavior was the strongest for the boys who started out being the most difficult—that is, they cried and fussed and were hardest to control as infants and toddlers. What this finding suggests, Belsky says, is that the children who try their parents' patience the most are those who stand to benefit most from patient, supportive parenting. And they have the most to lose from parents who regularly "lose it."

Show Boys Alternatives to Hitting and Other Kinds of Aggressive Behavior. Fathers, grandfathers, uncles, and other important men in a boy's life have an especially strong influence in taming a boy's aggressiveness in circumstances that are likely to provoke it. It helps boys to see these men using words, not fists, to settle an argument. And these men should coach boys on how to stand up for themselves without getting into physical fights at school.

Seek "Take Charge" Teachers. Elementary school teachers can have a long-term affect on their students' levels of aggression by doing something as basic as keeping the class under control. In a Johns Hopkins study, most of the boys who were aggressive in the first grade were also aggressive in the sixth grade. But the aggressive first-grade boys whose teachers effectively squelched disruptive behavior in the classroom became less aggressive by the sixth grade than did similar boys whose first-grade classes were more of a free-for-all. The researchers think that keeping the classroom well controlled inhibited these boys' aggressive behavior by toning down the overall aggression level of the class. The long-term effect was to help improve the boys' self-control.

Give Your Son Opportunities to Nurture. Nurturing is a hedge against aggressive behavior. "If you do a lot of nurturing, you become more nurturing," said Carol Nagy Jacklin. Boys have fewer chances to nurture, and they have more aggressive tendencies than do girls. But Jacklin thinks that parents can help shift the balance by giving their sons more chances to be caregivers and mentors. At the least, she suggests giving them pets to feed and tend to. But also hand them a baby sibling or cousin to hold and, when they're old enough, suggest that they find part-time jobs baby-sitting or working at a summer camp.

Limit Your Child's Exposure to Violence.   The leading cause of aggressive behavior in boys as well as girls is firsthand experience with violence: Being hit or in other ways physically abused, witnessing violent acts, and routinely seeing family members fight physically or verbally. Violent TV shows, movies, videos, and shoot-em-up computer games are also associated with violent behavior in children.

Don't Be Overprotective.   If your toddler whimpers when a neighbor approaches walking her dog, don't automatically pick your child up so that the dog won't frighten her. If your older child falls off her bike, help her get back on, even if she's a bit scared. In other words, don't be afraid to let your child be afraid. Jerome Kagan's research found that the high-reactive babies—those who tended to become fearful children—were less likely to become fearful and anxious later on if their mothers didn't shield them from run-of-the-mill stressful situations.

Set and Enforce Limits.   A common denominator of the low-fear children in Kagan's studies was that their parents (in this case, their mothers) set firm limits at home. The mothers were not harsh—they didn't yell or hit. But they blocked their toddlers from reaching forbidden objects and spoke sternly if the children misbehaved. Some of the mothers of high-reactive infants were lenient with them, perhaps out of fear that if the babies didn't get their way, they'd cry or throw tantrums. But permissiveness had the opposite effect with these children. Not knowing the limits scared these children, and it made them more fearful over time.

3

Gender Identity

Why Even Your Child Sometimes Acts
Like a Stereotypical Boy or Girl

BATMAN AND BARBIE

The scene is the fourth birthday party for brother and sister twins. It's one party with two themes revealing the binary world of preschool boys and girls. There's one set of plates, cups, napkins, and stickers with Batman and another set with Barbie. The twins' parents leave it up to the children to decide which plates, cups, and so on, they want, and make it clear that mixing and matching is OK. Some of the girls mix, but most go with Barbie all the way. None of the boys touches the Barbie stuff.

As one of the highlights, the children can have their pictures taken as either Batman or Barbie by standing behind a mounted blowup of the character with the face cut out. Some of the parents make halfhearted attempts to let their children think that they can be whichever character they'd like. One father, his hair in a ponytail, says to his daughter, "So, honey, do you want to be Batman or Barbie?" But to the children, there's really no choice. The girls line up behind Barbie, the boys behind Batman.

One of the biggest mysteries to parents is how their children come to act "like boys" or "like girls." The parents of these twins didn't set out to push Barbie on their daughter and Batman on their son. At first, they bought trucks and blocks and dolls and stuffed animals for both children. They enrolled them both in a dance class when they were 3. But despite the parents' earnest effort to avoid applying gender labels to toys and activities, guess what? Their children did the labeling. The girl played with the dolls, the boy with the trucks. The girl kept going to the dance class and the boy dropped out because he said it was for girls. She discovered Barbie, he discovered Batman. The parents threw up their hands and stopped trying to reroute their son's and daughter's interests.

Not all preschool boys and girls adhere as strictly to the boy script and the girl script as this brother and sister do. And even they, like most boys and girls, enjoy many of the same things: riding tricycles, playing on swings, reading Winnie the Pooh stories, and curling up with a favorite stuffed animal. But the experience of the twins' parents is replicated to varying degrees in households across the country where parents try to raise their children not to grow up believing the old, stifling gender stereotypes only to see their children embrace them. The stories that parents tell have become clichés: "I wouldn't buy him a gun, so he made one out of Tinker Toys." "I gave him a doll, but he refused to play with it." "She loves to wear pink frilly dresses, and I don't know where she gets it from—I live in jeans."

In the past thirty years, there's been a revolution in society's views on gender roles. Women have flooded the workplace, men have gotten more involved in child rearing, and parents and teachers have become more sensitive to gender-equity issues and tried harder to eliminate bias at home and in the classroom. The world has changed, but children, in many respects, haven't. Witness two studies that were done about thirty years apart. In 1963, the first study found that 97 percent of 6-year-old boys played with cars and other toy vehicles and just 51 percent of girls did. That study also found that 99 percent of 6-year-old girls and 17 percent of 6-year-old boys played frequently with dolls. More little girls have cars and trucks today, and more little boys have dolls, but they seem to be ignoring them. In 1994, another study found that the percentage of boys and girls who played with these toys was the same as it was in 1963.

This chapter explores the reasons why, despite the enormous social changes of recent decades, most children still play and think in gender-stereotyped ways. Many parents worry that gender stereotypes restrict children's ideas about themselves and their potential, as well as their opportunities for learning. But researchers on gender development—some of whom are parents who started out with these concerns—have a more relaxed view. In studying children at play, they've come to see that latching onto gender-typed behavior and attitudes helps children understand their gender identity, what it means to be a boy or a girl. To the extent that stereotypical behaviors are tied up with the healthy process of self-discovery, researchers consider them to be healthy, too.

Gender-stereotypical play is negative only if children are forced into it by parents and others who label certain activities as being for boys or for girls only. But children who are brought up without such restrictions gradually stop play-acting with extreme feminine and masculine behavior as they develop a firmer sense of who they are. And there are some encouraging signs that as society has shed many gender biases, more children are doing the same as they grow up.

THE "TRUCK GENE"

"My son has what our pediatrician calls the truck gene," said Fran, the mother of a 3-year-old boy and a 6-year-old girl in Maryland. "Anything he plays with becomes a truck. Give him two forks, he makes them into a truck. Give my daughter two forks, and she makes them into a bride and a groom."

No, there isn't really a truck gene. But one school of thought in the gender development field is that boys' and girls' preferences for different toys are, in part, biological, traced to differences in their brains created by the different levels of androgens they encountered in the womb. The theory goes as follows. The male brain is said to be more primed for action and aggression, so it should take less coaxing to interest boys in toys that move fast and can crash, like trucks and cars, than in sedate toys like dolls. The female brain, in contrast, is said to be more primed for nurturing and one-on-one communication, so it is more responsive to the toy props for this sort of behavior, such as dolls. Some support for this theory comes from studies of girls with AGS, a condition that results from overexposure to androgens in the womb. These girls, lo and behold, don't like dolls very much and do like trucks and cars.

Some studies have found that girls as young as 1 year old show a special interest in dolls and that boys turn away from dolls in favor of trucks, even when they have access to both kinds of toys. If this finding truly reflects the experiences of most infants, it means that girls and boys yearn for sex-typed toys long before they even know whether they're boys or girls, much less what boys and girls are. It suggests that when parents shop for their daughters in the "boy" aisle of a toy store and shop for their sons in the "girl" aisle, biology is sure to have the last laugh.

Watching her 1-year-old boy and girl twins made one mother wonder if biology might be snickering at her and her husband. In a letter to the editor in the *New York Times*, Stephanie McCavitt of New Jersey said that even though her children had access to the same toys, they played with different ones. "Our son gravitates to toys like building blocks and those that allow him to fit one thing inside another. Our daughter's face lights up at the sight of her dolls and she is much less aggressive," she wrote. "Based on my experience, it is incorrect to say that society is completely to blame for all differences between boys and girls."

It's hard to believe that most boys and girls really show such divergent interests so early. At 1, my son and daughter were different in many ways, but toy selection wasn't one of them. Both had a favorite stuffed bear, rolled balls across the floor, knocked down block towers, turned the knobs on their busy box, pulled the string on their toy phone to hear it play music and spun toy car wheels with their fingers. My daughter had two dolls, but she showed little interest in them.

My son didn't have any dolls until he was around 2, when he asked me to buy him one. I happily took him to Toys "R" Us, sure that we were breaking down the Berlin Wall of barriers to equal-opportunity play for boys and girls. When we got home, David promptly took the doll's clothes off, dismembered it, and abandoned it like road kill on the living room floor. He didn't play with it again.

It may not happen as early as 1, but researchers are certain of one thing: A significant number of boys and girls start to behave in sex-typed ways even before they become aware of their sex, which usually happens between ages 2 and 3. Many boys really do develop a thing for transportation toys and making sputtering motor sounds, and they tend to ignore dolls.

Many girls choose dolls and other feminine toys, like pretend kitchens. Whether there is a biological reason why boys and girls prefer different toys is debatable. But there are many factors at home and at school that steer very young boys and girls in divergent directions.

SOCIAL ENGINEERING BY PARENTS

It's hardly surprising that research has found that the children whose parents talk the most about what little girls and little boys do and don't do tend to play in sex-typed ways at the earliest ages. The parents praise their daughters for doing things like pretend-feeding their dolls and their sons for racing toy cars across the floor. And the parents give their children negative feedback for behaving in ways that are not considered appropriate for their sex. By making gender an important issue, these parents draw their children's attention to it early on, and as toddlers, at least, the children behave in more gender-stereotyped ways than other children do. But, of course, as the parents of the 4-year-old twins and other like-minded parents discover, most children eventually follow this learning curve no matter how hard parents soft-peddle the gender issue at home.

Parents who try to not to guide their children toward gender-typed toys and activities may not be trying as hard as they think. Fathers are especially touchy about their sons seeming too feminine as they get older. The father who clicks the camera in amusement as his 6-month-old son squeezes a doll shows less enthusiasm when his son is 1 or $1^1/_2$ years old. But it's not just fathers. Studies consistently find that both parents are less tolerant of feminine behavior in their sons than they are of masculine behavior in their daughters. Girls who play with Thomas the

Tank Engine are breaking free of traditional gender-stereotyped play, but boys who play with Madeline are what?—confused, strange, a little off? This double standard may help explain why boys show a preference for "boy" toys before girls show a preference for "girl" toys.

How do parents engineer their sons away from dolls, tea sets, and the like? The most obvious way is not to have them around. When my son, David, was 1½, he liked to play with the toy kitchen at my nieces' house. But when I suggested buying him one, my husband, a man even an ardent feminist could love, refused. We were both surprised to hear him say that he thought that a kitchen was an inappropriate toy for a boy. "Let's get him a toy tool bench instead," he said, referring to the more socially acceptable male analog of the kitchen.

But often the engineering is subtler. Parents may buy their son a toy kitchen, but not spend as much time helping him prepare imaginary meals as they do helping him build with blocks or throw a ball. One provocative study of parents who were trying to avoid sex typing their children's toys and activities looked at how well their beliefs meshed with their actions. The parents admitted that while they seldom told their sons not to play with dolls, they seldom encouraged them to play with dolls, either, whereas they did engage their daughters in doll play. And while parents openly discouraged both their sons and their daughters from playing with toy guns, they put their feet down harder with their daughters.

Parents not only encourage their children to play with gender-typed toys, they also play differently with their sons and daughters, which, in turn, could influence their sons' and daughters' toy preferences. Parents (especially fathers) play rougher with their sons and (especially mothers) talk more to their daughters almost from birth. If boys start out accustomed to being jiggled and bounced and fashioned into a human air-plane, it stands to reason that they may enjoy airplanes and foot-balls and other action toys. And if girls start out accustomed to face-to-face "conversation," it makes sense that they may feel comfortable with activities that lend themselves to talking and building relationships, like playing house or comforting a doll.

It seems obvious that the kinds of toys that parents give their children from infancy onward and the ways that parents treat their children should influence how gender stereotyped the children become. In other words, giving girls lots of frilly dresses and saying, "Oooh" and "Aahh," when they swaddle their dolls should make girls want pretty dresses and dolls. And discouraging boys from playing with dolls and toy kitchens should train boys to shun these things.

But here's where things get complicated. The relationship between what the parents and children do isn't straightforward. Beverly Fagot and Mary Leinbach, of the University of Oregon, tracked the attitudes of parents and the behavior of their chil-dren from the time the children were $1\frac{1}{2}$ years old until they were 4. The $1\frac{1}{2}$ year olds whose parents gave their the most encouragement to play with sex-typed toys were the first to label toys and other objects as being either for boys or for girls. At about $2\frac{1}{2}$, these early labelers played in the most gender-stereotyped ways—the girls showed a strong preference for dolls and other conventional girl toys, and the boys showed a strong preference for conventional boy toys. But by 4, the chil-dren whose parents had flexible attitudes toward play and behavior had caught up; as a group, they were every bit as sex typed as those whose parents had stereotypical attitudes. So, parents may not have much control over their children's ulti-mate preferences for toys.

Eleanor Maccoby and Carol Nagy Jacklin also found little

evidence that parents, however hard they may try, succeed in "raising" their young children to behave like either conventional or unconventional girls or boys. In their observations of children from infancy until about 4 years old, they said that the frequency with which parents offered their children sex-typed toys and engaged them in sex-typed play at age 4 was unrelated to the children's preferences for such toys and play when they were away from home. In other words, the boys who spent a lot of time racing Matchbox cars with their dads didn't necessarily favor the cars at nursery school. And the girls who had lots of dolls and doll accessories at home didn't necessarily make a beeline for the dolls at school.

With older children, when their parents give them gender-typed toys, it's not because the parents force such toys on them but because the children ask for them. In one particularly revealing study, researchers looked at the lists of toys that children requested in their letters to Santa Claus and compared them to the toys the children got for Christmas. Most of the toys on the lists were gender typed, and these made up 63 percent of the gifts they received.

Parents do influence the gender stereotyping of their children's play and attitudes. But many researchers now think that peers and society at large hold more sway.

SOCIAL ENGINEERING BY PEERS

From the time he could walk, Ross liked to wear the jellies that his older sister had outgrown. But that changed one summer day shortly before his second birthday when a 7-year-old girl from the neighborhood, seeing him in jellies, said, "Those are for *girls!*" Ross took them off and told his mother what the girl had said. Even though his mother said that it was OK for him to wear the jellies, Ross never put them on again.

Who says peer pressure is just for teenagers? For this 2 year old, another child's opinion carried more weight than his own mother's. Maybe this girl had exceptional power over Ross because she was older, and young children take their cues from older ones. But toddlers and preschoolers also influence children their own age. And where attitudes about gender are concerned, playmates seem more influential than parents.

In one study, researchers observed groups of children aged $1^1/_2$ to 4 during free play. At all ages, the girls smiled, played with, and in other ways rewarded other girls for playing dress-up or housekeeping, drawing, or engaging in other activities that were quiet, feminine, or both. The boys punished other boys—by ignoring them or teasing them—for doing these sorts of things, but gave one another positive feedback—laughing, cheering, or joining in—when they acted in traditionally male ways, such as playing with trucks or getting rambunctious. The caregivers praised all the children for doing artwork and other quiet play, but this praise had far less impact on the boys than on the girls. The girls toned down their behavior to please the caregivers, whereas the boys revved up their behavior to please their peers.

In another study, when pairs of 3- to 5-year-old boys were playing together and one boy picked up a feminine toy, the other boy would make fun of him and, in some cases, even hit him. When pairs of girls this age were playing and one picked up a masculine toy, the other girl usually ignored her. Though boys were actively punished and girls were merely ignored for playing with untraditional toys, the messages were similar: Playing with cross-sex toys won't score a preschooler points with his or her classmates.

At home, older siblings have a stronger hand in shaping a younger child's gender-related ideas and behavior than parents do. But what's fascinating about the influence of siblings is that it differs, depending on the number of siblings, their sex, and their birth order. In families with two children of the same sex, the older one appears to be a role model for the younger one. Carol Beal describes research on college students that found that women with older sisters were, on average, more feminine in a traditional sense than were other women and that boys with older brothers were more traditionally masculine. In families with a boy and a girl, the younger sibling tends to play in less stereotypical ways than his or her peers. Although a boy with an older sister doesn't necessarily push doll carriages, he may prefer gender-neutral toys like puzzles to boyish toys like action figures. And a girl with an older brother tends to be more athletic and active and to have a greater tolerance for getting dirty than other girls.

In families with three or more brothers and sisters, the influence of siblings is not so straightforward. Beal says that instead of automatically following in the footsteps of an older brother who plays football or an older sister who enjoys dancing, younger children try to carve out individual identities—the musician, the chess player, the animal lover. So the younger siblings are as likely to be conventionally sex typed as not. In families with three or more same-sex siblings, the youngest sister often rebels against the perceived femininity of the older sisters, and the youngest brother often bridles against the masculine behavior of the older brothers. So the youngest sister is more likely than the older ones to be a tomboy, and the younger brother is more likely to be quieter and openly nurturing than the older ones.

SOCIAL ENGINEERING BY SOCIETY

A teacher in Manhattan went into a toy store on Madison Avenue looking for a gift for a friend's 4-year-old son. Not knowing much about the child's interests, she asked the saleswoman to recommend some toys for children this age.

"Boy or girl?" the saleswoman asked.

"It's a 4 year old," the woman said. "Does it matter?"

"Well, some toys aren't appropriate for boys."

The customer expected the saleswoman to use dolls as an example, but much to her surprise the saleswoman pointed to a toy theater. "Boys don't usually like this," she said.

"But Shakespeare was a boy," said the shopper, in full-blown indignation.

She bought the theater and the little boy loved it.

Would the boy have loved the toy theater if someone had told him that most boys don't like it? That depends on the boy, but there's a good chance that he wouldn't have liked it as much. Gender-neutral toys and games appeal to both boys and girls. Think of popular items like puzzles, puppets, movie viewers, and ring toss and games like Candyland, Chutes and Ladders, and Uno. But a child's enthusiasm for one of these things can be snuffed out in an instant if it is shown in a commercial or in a movie being used only by children of the other sex or if it's shelved in the other-sex aisle of a toy store.

No child leaves childhood without being told that some toy or activity is for boys or for girls. Even if parents are careful not to use such labels, other adults in a child's life probably aren't. There may be a well-meaning but old-fashioned nursery school teacher who shepherds a 3-year-old boy away from the dress-up area. Or a grandmother who says of her granddaughter, "Look at her throw! She's as good as the boys." Or a parent at the local playground who, seeing a little boy take the pink bucket lying unused in the sandbox, says, "Don't use the pink one. That's for a girl." These sorts of messages are in the air and, of course, on the airwaves.

On TV, commercials for dolls and dollhouses show pretty girls sporting long, curled hair and party dresses as soft music plays in the background. Flashing robots and voice-command trucks are operated by daredevil boys sporting devilish grins to the beat of loud music. Several studies have found a strong relationship between the amount of TV a child watches and how stereotyped the child's views are about boys and girls. And TV commercials certainly influence children's ideas about which toys are right for them.

Consider a study done with young children and a movie viewer, a toy that normally appeals to boys and girls. Two groups watched a movie with a commercial for a toy movie viewer. One group saw a commercial with a boy using the viewer, the other with a girl. Afterward, all the children, whose ages ranged from $3^1/_2$ to $6^1/_2$, were given the chance to play with a toy movie viewer. Most of the preschoolers played with it regardless of which commercial they saw; they were too young to understand the gender subtext. But the most of the schoolchildren were hypersensitive to it. They wouldn't play with the viewer if they'd seen the commercial with the child of the other sex.

Some retailers are trying to counter these messages with gender-neutral or even gender-bending messages of child's play. Childcraft, the toy catalog, shows a toddler boy and girl crouched over a doll in a cradle bedecked with white and pink ruffles. On other pages, a toddler boy is playing alone with a dollhouse, and a girl who looks about 5 is constructing a locomotive out of Lego-type building shapes. But until most toy catalogs, stores, and people in general stop segregating toys by gender, dollhouses will continue to be bought mainly for girls and building toys for boys.

GENDER IDENTITY

Sometime between their second and third birthdays, most children can point to themselves and say "I am a boy" or "I am a girl" and can identify (although not always accurately) the sex of other children. This milestone, called gender awareness, marks the beginning of children's long, persistent effort to figure out what it means to be a boy or a girl. Children's awareness of the sexes works much the same way as their awareness of different colors (which is emerging at the same time). Once they can tell red from blue, they start to separate, say, the blue blocks from the red blocks. Once they can tell boys from girls, they begin to mentally separate how boys and girls dress and what kinds of things they do and play with. Indeed, children's awareness of color and gender intersect. In one study, 2- to 3 year olds said that pink and lavender were "girl" colors and brown and blue were "boy" colors.

Children gather information about boys and girls in many ways and from many sources: by observing other children; watching videos and TV; looking at the decorations in their bedrooms; and, of course, listening to what their parents and other adults tell them. As children take all these details in, the sex differences in their play and behavior increase. Many children also gravitate more toward same-sex playmates, especially at school or day care where there's a choice of children to play with. (Otherwise, they'll take any child—the one next door or down the block or at the playground.) As their gender awareness increases, boys become more active and boisterous, on average, than girls. Many girls who'd thus far seemed blithely genderless in their pursuits— looking for worms in the garden, playing ball, and linking magnetic toy freight cars to engines—suddenly want to wear party dresses and jewelry. These girls don't necessarily abandon their old activities, but now they may dress for them in spangled bracelets and tutus. Parents who had considered their children to be pretty much androgynous now begin to think, "Gee, he's a real boy now" or "She's such a girl."

It isn't until children are about 6 when they progress from having gender awareness to gender constancy—fully understanding that boys remain boys and grow up to be men and girls remain girls and grow up to be women. The further along children are, the more sensitive they become to the messages about which toys, activities, and clothing are "for girls" or "for boys." They're apt to show special interest in a new toy if they're told it's for their sex, even if the item doesn't seem to have anything to do with gender.

A study similar to the one involving the TV commercial for the toy movie viewer showed just how strong the power of suggestion is in influencing schoolchildren's attitudes about toys. In the study, children aged 6 to 8 were introduced to a game that involved throwing marbles into the body of a toy clown that spun around on a rod. The researchers described the game differently to different groups of the children. They told one group that it was "a toy for boys, like basketball." They told another group that it was "a toy for girls, like jacks." And they told yet another group simply that it was a new toy but didn't say anything about gender. The children who thought the game was appropriate for their sex showed more interest in it, said it was more fun, and actually played it better than the other children. The children who were told that the toy was for the other sex showed the least interest in it.

It can be disheartening for parents to hear their children declare that they no longer play with an interesting toy because they think it is for children of the other sex. My daughter has always loved building with blocks. It's often the first thing she does when she comes home from school. When she was 3, her teacher told me that she spent much of her free-play time building houses and roads out of blocks. But just shy of her fifth birthday, her attitude toward blocks changed.

One night at dinner she said, out of the blue, "Guess who plays with the blocks at school, the girls or the boys?"

"I don't know," I said.

"The boys."

"Really," I said. "But you like to play with blocks. Do you play with blocks at school?"

"Sometimes I help the boys."

She *helps* the boys! What was I supposed to say? That she shouldn't play second fiddle to the boys because she can build magnificently on her own? I was afraid that my lecture would bore her or, worse, that it would backfire. If I told her that girls shouldn't think of themselves as boys' helpers, would I put the idea in her mind that girls are inferior to boys?

I spared us both the lecture and simply asked, "What do the girls play with at school?"

"Play-Doh, art, dress-up."

BARBIES AND GUNS: WORTH A BATTLE?

Many parents regard blocks and some of the other toys that boys tend to play with as being fundamentally more interesting and educational than the toys girls play with. These parents worry that if their daughters don't play with such toys, their development and their shot at gender equity will suffer. Building with blocks and Legos, for example, works children's spatial skills, so if girls don't build things—either because they don't have building toys or because they think these toys are for boys— the fear is that they will lack spatial skills and face a life-long disadvantage as a result. Spatial skills are related to math skills, and math skills are prerequisites for succeeding in school and entering many high-paid careers.

That's an awful lot of responsibility to hang on individual toys. Is it warranted? Probably not. While some toys help develop particular skills, "there's no proof that playing with certain toys will give boys and girls a certain edge academically," says Beal, who has been working on ways to bolster girls' interest and achievement in math. Beal says she was not at all displeased when her 3-year-old daughter started wanting to play dress-up. "The work I've done taught me that it's part of her trying to figure out who she is," she says. "I took it as a sign of normal development."

Jeri Jaeger was not so philosophical when her children were young. As a scientist at the University of Buffalo who studies differences between males' and females' brains, she was disappointed when her two daughters ignored the trucks and other "boy" toys she offered them and when her son ignored the dolls. "I was really upset that I couldn't get my kids to be gender neutral," she says. But now that they're teenagers, she sees no long-term damage, based on their academic records and challenging extracurricular pursuits. She's learned that what's most important to nurturing children's development is for parents to support their children's interests.

Beal points out that many of the toys that girls enjoy are more educational than parents think. Play-Doh, art supplies, dress-up clothes, and paper dolls have a lot to recommend them. They involve creativity and imagination. Play-Doh, drawing and painting, and paper dolls work a child's fine-motor skills and spatial ability. Dress-up uses gross- and fine-motor skills, as well as verbal and social skills (girls talk as they primp and act out fantasy scenes).

But what about gender-specific toys that have no apparent educational or socially redeeming value, like Barbies and guns?

No two toys separate the girls from the boys as much as Barbies and guns do. They epitomize toys that promote gender-stereotyped attitudes in girls and boys, and for that reason, they set off alarm bells in parents' minds. Some mothers talk about Barbies as if they were cocaine. "I tried to keep them out of the house, but as soon as my daughter started day care and saw the other girls with them, she had to have one," said one New York mother about her 2 year old. "She begged me to buy her one. She threw a tantrum in the store. What could I do?" Other mothers feel the need to explain their daughters' Barbie collection by saying things like: "We didn't buy any of them. They were all gifts." Of course, still other mothers are cavalier, reasoning that Barbies are like a little dessert on a smorgasbord of weightier offerings, such as dance classes, music lessons, and educational software.

Toy guns may lack the appeal that they once had among boys, now that there are so many video games that let them blow away an enemy by pressing a button. But many children—mainly boys—still like them, and many parents deliberate about whether to buy toy guns as if they were making a political statement, which, in a sense, they are. I remember the mother of a 4-year-old boy in my son's nursery school class apologizing for having laserlike toy guns in her house, which both of our sons were enjoying immensely. "He's my second," she said kind of sheepishly. "You know, you give in more with the second child."

Even though parents have only limited influence over the toys that their children fall in love with, they inevitably wonder if they can (or should) discourage (or forbid) their children from playing with toys that seem to invite sexist behavior. If you want your daughter to be intellectually curious and physically active, do you really want her spending her time admiring Barbie's lustrous hair, improbably thin waist, and stylish clothes? If you want your son to be more sensitive, should you give him props for pretending to blow someone's brains out?

The overwhelming opinion from gender researchers is, let your kids have Barbies and guns if they really want them. Playing with Barbie dolls will not prevent your daughter from becoming a brain surgeon or a lawyer, and shooting toy guns will not bar your son from becoming a music composer or a minister. "I owned more than 20 Barbie dolls in my youth and grew up, nevertheless, to attend Yale Law School and work as a litigator on Wall Street," a woman wrote in a letter to the *New York Times*. But psychologists also suggest talking to your children about the downside of these toys.

"The best thing you can do is accept your child's interest while, at the same time, informing your child why you have some problems with it," said Robyn Fivush of Emory University. "If Barbie is having a wedding, you might say, 'Isn't that nice that Barbie's planning her wedding. But what else is she going to do?'" Eleanor Maccoby recommends not sweating the toy gun issue, but she says that parents should talk to their sons, as well as their daughters, about the dangers of real guns.

"IF I WERE A GIRL, I'D HAVE TO ATTRACT A GUY"

It's one thing to be philosophical when your children want sex-typed toys. But what do you do when they spout sexist views—the very biases that you as a parent have worked hard to disprove? Carol Nagy Jacklin described an experience that one of her former students had taking her preschool daughter to school on a bus in Manhattan. The little girl remarked that her mother was the only woman on the bus who wasn't wearing makeup and then said that she should wear makeup because she would look prettier. This girl's mother didn't raise her to associate makeup with beauty. Where did this thought come from?

Young children are the most gender-biased people on the planet. They look for details that set males and females apart: how they dress, how their hair looks, how they talk, the things they do. If mom does most of the cooking, then women cook. If dad mows the lawn, then men mow. If all the longhaired children at school are girls, then only girls have long hair. If the heroes in books and videos are mostly males, then males are brave. Though recent books, movies, and computer games have made progress in portraying strong, courageous female characters, there's enough older entertainment out there to perpetuate the stereotypes of females as helpless and dependent on males and of males as being heroes.

It's as if children carry two buckets, one for male characteristics and the other for female characteristics, and whatever goes into one bucket can't go into the other. Young children are inflexible on this point. The notion that both boys and girls can have long hair, for instance, is too confusing for a 4 year old to grasp. Through preschool and into elementary school, children modify their lists of stereotypes somewhat to reflect their expanded knowledge. They delete some items but add others.

It goes without saying that children are as biased as the culture around them. Studies conducted in Europe have found that children in countries, such as Holland, where gender roles are among the most flexible, hold fewer gender stereotypes than children in countries, such as Italy, where women are expected to serve men.

As parents, we have only limited power to change our culture. But parents do matter. Research shows that schoolchildren who are raised in households where both parents work hold less traditional views about gender roles than do children whose mothers stay at home, although the effect is greater for daughters than for sons of working women. But whether or not a mom works isn't the only factor. What counts is whether the parents truly practice the egalitarian values that they preach. Does dad cook and do laundry? Does Mom troubleshoot computer glitches? Do Mom and Dad share the child care duties equally? Do the parents really believe that boys and girls can pursue the same interests, and do they hold their sons and daughters to the same high standards?

A few years ago, Barbara Risman, a professor of sociology at North Carolina State University, set out to study such families to see how successful the parents were at passing along their views to their children. Finding truly egalitarian families was hard, but after an extensive search in North Carolina, she found 15 to participate in her study. Among them they had 12 boys and 9 girls, ranging in age from 4 to 15. In the course of interviewing these children, Risman and her colleagues found that all but 2 really believed that men and women were equal or ought to be. And even those 2, both 4 year olds, had views that Risman described as inconsistent instead of traditional. None of the 4-to 6 year olds thought that boys and girls had different personalities and interests, a radical departure from the highly stereotypical views expressed in other studies by most of the children in this age group from more mainstream households.

But as far as the older children were concerned, men and women were more equal than boys and girls. Nearly all the children aged 7 and older still embraced their parents' beliefs that men and women should be free to work in any occupation and that household chores should not be divided according to sex.

But these children used the familiar gender stereotypes to describe their peers: They said that girls were sweet and neat; that boys were athletic, competitive, and disruptive; and so on. "The children voiced unequivocal belief in major sex differences between boys and girls just minutes after parroting their parents' feminist views about the equality and similarity of men and women," Risman wrote in her book, *Gender Vertigo*.

What accounted for the difference? Three of the children in the study tried to explain. For example, an 8-year-old boy said that he knew that girls could be into sports or computers, but he didn't know any girls who were. Clearly, the values that these children learned at home were at odds with what they saw and heard when they were with their peers. And when push came to shove, peers were more influential. Risman cited a 6-year-old boy in the study who said that if a magician were to turn him into a girl, he'd be different because he would have long hair. That was a curious thing for this particular boy to say, since his father wore his hair in a ponytail and his mother wore her hair short.

Though they were weaned on gender equity, these children, like others, came to see that males have the power in our society. This point comes through in the following poem, which an 8-year-old boy wrote when asked what it would be like to be a girl. One can only imagine how his feminist parents must have felt upon reading it:

If I were a girl I'd have to attract a guy
Wear makeup; sometimes.
Wear the latest styles of clothes and try to be likable.
I probably wouldn't play any physical sports like football or soccer.
I don't think I would enjoy myself around men
In fear of rejection
Or under pressure of attracting them.

Did the parents of this boy and the other children in the study fail? No. In fact, Risman looks at these children and actually sees progress. She explains their contradictory views— that they applied gender stereotypes mainly to their peers, not to adults—as symptoms of "gender vertigo," her phrase for the confusion someone feels when his or her ideas about gender evolve faster than the prevailing ideas in the culture. Risman is confident that these children will outgrow their stereotypical views and come to see them as childish, like a taste for sticky sweets. In the more complex world of college and career preparation, they will realize that gender-neutral behavior like hard work serve them a lot better than simplistic notions about males and females. Just as mom and dad said.

If recent reports from the world beyond gender-egalitarian families are any indication, Risman's utopia may become reality. One 1994 study found that sixth graders were twice as likely as kindergartners to believe that boys and girls can, or should, engage in a variety of activities. The important point here is that as they got older, more children believed that gender should not restrict boys and girls in pursuing their interests. Eleanor Maccoby notes that girls in particular are less inclined than they once were to assume that certain activities and occupations are for males or females. "These findings may indicate that efforts to expand the horizons of children's thinking about possible roles for the two sexes have born some fruit," she wrote in *The Two Sexes*.

BOY-GIRL FRIENDSHIPS: A RARE BREED

Even as children's views of gender roles become more flexible over time, their views on friendships remain fairly rigid. During any given school recess period from preschool through middle school, there are groups of girls playing together and groups of boys playing together. Of course, there are boys and girls playing together, too. And boys will make forays into girls' groups, and vice versa. But most of the children spend most of their time with playmates of their own sex, and this separation becomes more distinct as children progress from preschool to elementary school and from elementary school to middle school. Children also separate into racial and ethnic groups, but sex is a stronger factor. Given a choice of playing with a child of a different race and the same sex or the same race and the other sex, a child will join the classmate of the same sex.

In a study of 100 children in different preschools in the San Francisco Bay Area, Maccoby and Jacklin found that the children spent nearly three times as much time with children of their sex than with children of the other sex. When the children were 6^1/$_2$, they spent eleven times as much time with children of their own sex. Around the world, anthropologists have found basically the same pattern, although the degree of separation varies from place to place. Maccoby calls playmate preference one of the strongest gender differences.

Many parents whose children used to play happily with both boys and girls wonder why their children are no longer gender blind. When 4^1/$_2$-year-old Chloe was invited to two parties on the same day, one for a boy in her class and the other for a girl in her neighborhood, her parents asked her which party she wanted to go to. She said, "I'm going to Hannah's party because she's a girl."

Is sex segregation normal and healthy? Or is it a sign of gender bias at school or at home? Do the children separate because they want to or because teachers and parents or other caregivers urge them, perhaps unconsciously, into different activities?

It looks as though boys and girls play separately because

they enjoy different toys and activities. After all, in preschool, many boys cluster in the block area and many girls flock to the housekeeping area. But toy and activity preferences don't seem to constitute the firewall that separates boys and girls. If they did, you'd expect children to show preferences for toys first, then soon afterward gravitate toward same-sex playmates. But that's not what happens. Many girls prefer playing with other girls by around age 2, before they show a marked interest in playing with things like toy kitchens and tea sets. With boys, the reverse is true—they tend to prefer sex-typed toys earlier than girls do, by around age 2, but they don't favor playing with other boys until they're 3 or 4 or even older.

By about age 4, many boys and girls show a definite preference for sex-typed toys and activities *and* same-sex playmates. But those who show a strong preference for one aren't necessarily the same ones who show a strong preference for the other. For further evidence that toys and activities aren't the crucial factor that divides boys and girls, one need look no farther than the local playground. Boys and girls all enjoy the swings, slides, monkey bars, and riding toys, but many of the children playing on them still group themselves by sex. There may be a few girls on the swings and a group of boys going down the slide.

Many parents think that children play with others of their sex because their parents, nannies, or teachers encourage them to do so. "I remember back when my daughter was in nursery school seeing the mothers of girls make play dates with girls and the mothers of boys make play dates with boys," said Shari, the mother of an 8-year-old girl. "I let my daughter play with whomever she liked, and one of her best friends was a boy. They're still good friends."

There's no question that adults influence children's choices of playmates. Researchers like Barrie Thorne who've done fieldwork on playgrounds have seen playground aides at elementary schools separate the girls from the boys during recess on many occasions. A group of girls may be playing jump rope or hop-scotch on the blacktop near where the playground aides usually stand. If some boys walk over, the aides frequently tell them to go away, assuming (based on experience) that the boys will soon start teasing the girls or disrupting their game.

But Thorne observes that even though the aides sometimes enforce the boy-girl separation, they don't create it. Nor do teachers, parents, or caregivers. Although some parents may avoid inviting boys over to play with their daughters even if their daughters want to play with boys, or vice versa, it's more often the case that parents make play dates with the children their children like best. Laura, the mother of 4-year-old Claire, said, "I used to make play dates with boys, but Claire only wants to play with girls now."

The bottom line is that when boys play with boys and girls play with girls, it's mainly because they want to, not because adults are separating them. As Thorne and other researchers have observed, sex segregation is most pronounced when chil-dren's activities are least structured and supervised by adults, such as during recess or free play and at lunchtime in school. One day, while watching second graders file into the cafeteria for lunch at a California pubic school, Thorne noticed a popular boy walk past a table that had a smattering of boys and girls. The boy said loudly, "Oooo, too many girls," then he sat at another table. The boys at the first table then moved, and no other boys sat at that table.

What makes many boys and girls want to sit at different tables and cluster in separate areas of the playground? Do they really dis-like each other? Are they so different at this point that they have little in common? Or are they just afraid of being teased?

TEASING

"It's hard for girls and boys to stay friends," Amy, a sixth grader, said to Barrie Thorne, as quoted in Thorne's book, *Gender Play.*

"Why?"

"I guess because boys are afraid other boys will call them sissy or say they have a crush on a girl."

There's no question that a powerful force that keeps elementary school boys and girls apart is the fear of being teased. A boy and a girl hanging out together on the playground are fair game for a group of children to giggle, point at, and accuse of being in *love.* Thorne met elementary school students who had good friends of the other sex whom they played with outside school but barely acknowledged in school because they didn't want to be teased.

Is it the teasing that causes the separation, or vice versa? That's a chicken-and-egg question. Teasing may force boy-girl friendships underground, but the rarity of boy-girl friendships also helps prompt the teasing. By about second grade, it's so unusual for boys and girls to play together that the sight of some of them actually doing it, on a regular basis, in public, probably makes many children feel uneasy. It may even upset their ideas about gender-appropriate behavior, which adds to their confusion. How do children act when they feel uncomfortable or confused? One way is to make wisecracks.

There's another factor. Children know that boys and girls don't play apart forever. Preadolescent and pre-preadolescent children look ahead and see older boys and girls hanging out together and dating. And, of course, there's mom and dad. So they may figure that the only reason why males and females could possibly be friends is that they're in love, certainly a tease-worthy idea to a young schoolchild.

What about preschool children? Teasing boys and girls for playing together is less common among preschoolers than it is among older children, but it happens. Perhaps it's part of their preparation for kindergarten, like learning to sound out letters and leave their "transitional objects" in their cubbies. One morning after I'd dropped my daughter off at nursery school, I heard a group of her classmates chanting, "Ricky is in lo-ove. Ricky is in lo-ove." The teasing surprised me, since Ricky, along with a few other boys in the class, regularly and openly played with girls. I scanned the playground and saw Ricky sitting under a tree with Michaela. Neither of them looked bothered by the teasing, but I couldn't help but wonder how long it would take for such teasing to drive them apart. Even in the beginning of the school year, most of the children in the class separated by sex, but the number of boy-girl friendships dwindled from September to June.

DIFFERENT PLAY STYLES

If teasing about boy-girl friendships isn't a major factor among 3 and 4 year olds, what makes many children this young begin to prefer playmates of their sex? Eleanor Maccoby and other psychologists who've spent a lot of time observing children think that the crucial factor is that boys and girls this age develop different styles of playing and that these styles make them more compatible and comfortable with same-sex playmates. Many boys enjoy mock-fighting, tackling, wrestling, and other forms of rough-and-tumble play. Rough play sometimes gets out of hand and turns aggressive, which leads to another trait that's more characteristic of boys' play than of girls': hitting and pushing. Still another aspect of male play might be called the "size matters" attitude. Boys often try to dominate one another by showing off their strength, skill, and toughness. Most young boys don't hold extended conversations with playmates, and when they do vocalize, it's often to growl or to yell in an attempt to control a group.

Girls' play style, while not exactly the opposite of boys', is less rough and aggressive and more conversational. Conversation is a key element—girls talk with their friends as they play, and even when playing alone they can often be heard inventing an elaborate dialogue between two dolls or toy figures. Girls' play more often involves nurturing themes: pretend-feeding dolls, comforting stuffed animals, and covering dolls or toy animals with blankets.

Boys and girls both engage in fantasy play, but the themes they act out underscore their different play styles. Boys' fantasy play often involves some superhero like Batman or Power Rangers or warriors like Darth Vader. They punch, kick (if only just the air), and wield guns or swords to vanquish an enemy. If their parents don't allow toy "weapons" in the house, boys will make their own out of sticks, discarded paper-towel rolls, or whatever other materials are at hand. In one study, boys engaged in mock combat or other playfully aggressive acts twice as often as girls at age 4 and six times as often at ages 5 to 8. Boys often act out fantasy fights with other boys, but they're just as likely to do their swashbuckling solo.

Girls' fantasy play is much more cooperative. Two girls will get together and assume a different character to act out a scene. If another child isn't around, the role of understudy may go to Mom or Dad. Sometimes, the scene has a domestic theme, such as a mommy and a daddy getting food for their baby, or a romantic theme with princesses or ballerinas. But videos and books can provide material, as well. Janet, an editor in Manhattan, recalls her preschool daughter greeting her when she came home from work with a request to help her play-act a scene from *The Wizard of Oz,* one of her favorite videos.

At this point, many parents are probably thinking, "*My* son doesn't go around wrestling other boys to the ground" and "What about my daughter? You should see her run around and get wild with other kids."

A few clarifications about play styles are in order. Describing play styles as either male or female leaves the false impression that all boys have a lock on the male one and all girls have a lock on the female one. But that's not what parents see or what the research shows. There's more variation between the way any two boys or any two girls play than there is between the ways that boys and girls play. Most boys' and girls' play is a blend of both styles, albeit tilted more toward one or the other. Take rough-and-tumble play, for instance. In one study of preschoolers, 15 percent to 20 percent of the boys scored higher than *any* of the girls on a measure of rough-and-tumble play, but the remaining 80 percent to 85 percent of the boys engaged in about the same degree of rough play as the girls. So, rough-and-tumble play is not an exclusively male trait.

In the real world, the differences in boys' and girls' play comes out in ways that are unique to each child. Just shy of her fifth birthday, my daughter, Sarah, loves playing basketball with her 8-year-old brother, David, and she'll do anything to get the ball away from him. I've seen her wrestle with him and try to punch the ball out of his hands, and when she gets it, she clutches it tight to keep him from getting it back. She plays rough and hard.

But other aspects of Sarah's play have a deeply nurturing quality that sets her apart from the boys. Sarah, David, and Sarah's friend Michael all collect Beanie Babies, but consider the different ways that they play with them. Sarah covers hers with blankets and tucks them into bed. She dresses them up.

Sometimes she asks for a cup of milk that she can "feed" to her cat Beanies. David often plays catch with his Beanie Babies. And Michael has devised a game in which he lines up his toy dinosaurs and throws Beanies at them to knock them over. Sarah loves dinosaurs, too, but she doesn't ambush them. She groups them into families of a mother, a father, and a baby or two, sometimes with a plastic egg that has a tiny dinosaur inside.

Whether Sarah's play will become even more nurturing and less rough in the years ahead remains to be seen. But if David's pattern is any indication, Sarah's play will become more like the other girls'. When David was her age, his play had more "female" qualities than it does now, $3\frac{1}{2}$ years later. His idea of a good time wasn't to play-fight, but to play a board game or just talk. He played with girls as often as he played with boys. Now, he rarely plays with girls. His idea of a good time is to play ball, hard and competitively, with a group of boys. His talk about these games is focused on who are the best players, who got a hit, and who cheated. But though his play style is more male, he he can still outtalk any girl.

GIRL SNUBS BOY, BOY REJECTS GIRL

Girls decide that they don't want to play with boys before boys decide that they don't want to play with girls. Many girls as young as 2 will cluster with other girls in school or day care, at least a year earlier than many boys start to gravitate toward other boys. Maccoby thinks that the girls make the first move because they're put off by the roughness and aggressiveness of many of the boys. When girls also avoid the quieter boys, it may well be because of guilt by association.

In the 2's class of a nursery school in suburban New York,

there was a boy who played especially rough. He'd grab toys and sometimes shove and boss around other children. He was popular among the boys, which makes sense, since research shows that boys are aroused by rough-and-tumble play even if they don't join in the jousting and wrestling. But many of the girls were afraid of him. Occasionally, they'd talk about him, saying things like, "He's mean" and "I don't like him." So this boy got a bad reputation among the girls, and most of them stayed away from him.

Even as the girls are snubbing the boys, most boys remain open to playing with girls (as well as with other boys) until they're 3 or older. Maccoby has a provocative explanation. Boys like playing with girls for the same reasons that girls like playing with girls: They're relatively easy to play with. They tend to listen when spoken to and not to spoil a good time by starting a fistfight. But as time passes, boys find girls' play too tame and boys' play too thrilling to pass up. So gradually more and more of the boys start playing together, with fewer and fewer girls.

The different play styles of boys and girls are most apparent when they're playing in single-sex groups. An individual boy and an individual girl together may not seem all that dissimilar in their behavior. Depending on their age, they may chat briefly about things like their favorite foods or an upcoming holiday, play cards or a computer game, go swimming, or play on the swings. But put that boy in a group of other boys and that girl in a group of other girls and see the small differences grow.

So the different play styles of boys and girls are both the causes and the effects of their separation. Having different play styles seems to make boys and girls want to play in separate groups in the first place, and playing in separate groups heightens their differences.

But where do boys' and girls' play styles come from? To

some extent, they are the products of nature, as fundamentally male or female as ovaries and testes. Yet play styles aren't as binary and fixed as sex organs. They can take on different characteristics, depending on how children are nurtured at home and the attitudes they encounter everywhere they go—at school, in the sandbox, in the movies, and on TV.

REASONS FOR DIFFERENT PLAY STYLES

The Nature Component

Children aren't the only ones who do it. Young monkeys and apes also spend more time with playmates of their own sex. Male rhesus monkeys that are 1 year old (the age equivalent of 4-year-old boys) hang out with other male yearlings and distance themselves from their mothers and sisters. Like boys, they play-fight. They tussle and wrestle with others their age about three times as often as females do. The females remain close to their mothers and other females. They spend time grooming the other females, as well as flocking around infants. The fact that human children and their evolutionary cousins start to separate themselves by sex at roughly the same stage in development suggests that biology is at work, in particular, sex differences in the brain.

No one has yet been able to point to a particular structure in the brain and say, "That's why males play rough" or "That's why females play house." But many scientists now think that there's got to be *something* about the brains of boys and girls (and young male and female animals) that explains their different play styles, as well as their impulse to avoid the other sex much of the time. Researchers think that prenatal exposure to relatively high levels of androgens somehow primes the male brain to be excited by rough, high-energy play and to react aggressively when pro-voked. And relatively low prenatal levels of androgens somehow prime the female brain to respond to opportunities to nurture. The effect of this priming doesn't reveal itself until months and years after birth as the brain develops and the child interacts with the world beyond the crib.

The strongest evidence of the priming theory comes from experiments with primates. Female primates whose mothers were injected with androgens during pregnancy play more roughly than other females. By the same token, in recent exper-iments in which newborn male rhesus monkeys were given a drug that blocked androgen activity, the males went on to behave more like females in one respect: They stayed close to their mothers even after the other males had begun spending more time with one another (and having more chances to play rough). So, high androgen exposure before or soon after birth seems to be a critical factor that influences the play styles and behavior that emerge years after birth. Other evidence comes from observations of girls born with AGS, a congenital disorder that leads to the absorption of excessive amounts of androgens before birth. Throughout their childhood, these girls play more like boys than like girls.

It also stands to reason that girls and boys play differently because they mature at different rates, with girls being more advanced in language skills and self-control (see Chapter 1, pages 23–29). A 2-year-old girl may be expressing herself in compound sentences when a boy her age can barely put two words together. So, it's easy to see why that girl may have trou-ble talking with a boy—she talks, and he doesn't respond or doesn't do as she asks. If she can't communicate with him, she may find him uninteresting or unappealing as a playmate.

The Nurture Component

Male and female play styles may have biological roots, but they're also nurtured at home. To a large extent, children do unto their peers as their parents do unto them.

Recall that parents, especially fathers, play more roughly with their sons than with their daughters from infancy onward. Parents also behave in what psychologists characterize as more "power-assertive" ways with their sons, meaning that they punish them by yelling at them and hitting them more often than they do their daughters. It's not that parents set out to be mean to their sons. Boys misbehave more (possibly by virtue of their relative lag in self-control) and respond less to verbal commands (possibly because of their lag in verbal skills). So, parents may feel that they have no choice but to turn up their own volume when their sons ignore even-toned no's and don'ts.

With their daughters, parents spend less time doing things like tossing a football than simply sitting and talking. In a recent study, Campbell Leaper and his colleagues at the University of California at Santa Cruz found that the difference in talking time was greatest during the toddler years. The timing is significant, they wrote, because the toddler years are "both the period of greatest language learning as well as the time when children's gender identity and gender role knowledge are being formed." Whatever the reasons why parents treat their sons and daughters differently, it's easy to see why, as they move from the stroller into the sandbox and from the sandbox into school, boys would be more comfortable with rough, power-assertive play and girls with quieter, more conversational play. These are the play styles they know best.

Boys and girls throughout the world separate into same-sex groups much of the time, but the degree of separation varies from child to child and from culture to culture. In their study of children and families from Africa, Asia, India, Mexico, and the United States, Beatrice Blyth Whiting, an anthropologist at Harvard, and Carolyn Pope Edwards, a professor of family studies at the University of Kentucky, made a provocative discovery. Boys' separation from females is the greatest in societies where men enjoy the highest status. So, it seems that separation is related to sexism.

In our society, though girls separate themselves from boys first, boys separate from girls with more vengeance. Many boys come to reject girls. One of the strongest insults one boy can hurl at another is to call him a *girl*. It's much less common for girls to put each other down by saying, "You're a boy!" This striking difference in attitude is not biological; it's societal. Barrie Thorne and Eleanor Maccoby think that one of the main reasons why boys reject girls and scorn anything that seems like girlish behavior in a boy is that they come to see that males— and masculine behavior—have a higher status.

Children catch on pretty early that males have more power than females. Many need only look at their own families, in which dad works and mom stays home and serves him dinner or mom and dad both work but mom still does most of the serving and household chores. Recent studies show that even though more than half of all mothers of young children work, mothers still do more household chores than fathers.

In addition, children learn that there's a pecking order to masculine and feminine activities and personality characteristics. Parents and society as a whole applaud when girls do traditionally male things, like play baseball or take chess classes. More than in the past, people also think it's a good idea for boys to get in touch with their feminine side and their feelings. But, for all the enlightened talk, researchers still find that parents approve more of their daughters than their sons making forays across gender lines. Girls who play sports or assert themselves with a bossy friend or build elaborate structures with Legos are seen as strong and smart. Boys who cry or complain arouse concern that they're weak and, let's face it, effeminate. The message is clear—masculine traits are better than feminine traits.

Many studies show that parents try to rid their sons of behavior that may be construed as feminine and that this pressure comes mainly from fathers. In one study of preschoolers and their parents, fathers were five times as likely to show disapproval when their sons played with a traditionally female toy, such as a dollhouse or a kitchen, as when their daughters played with a traditionally male toy like an army set. The mothers in this study were not biased: They were no more disturbed by their sons playing with girl toys than by their daughters playing with boy toys. But at best, the mothers and fathers were giving their sons mixed messages on which toys—and play styles—were appropriate.

Studies also show that parents discourage boys from expressing their feelings. Mothers spend much less time talking about emotions with their sons than with their daughters, giving sons less opportunity to reveal their fears and frustrations (see Chapter 2, pages 72–77). Fathers take a more proactive approach. When their sons cry or vent their feelings, many fathers are quick to tell them, in effect, to stop being such sissies.

The following brief interchange between a mother and a father speaks volumes about parents' attitudes toward their sons' crying. It was recorded in a research paper presented at a meeting of the American Society for Research in Child Development in 1993. The parents' toddler son had just fallen and hurt himself.

MOTHER: "Come here, honey. I'll kiss it better."
FATHER: "Oh, toughen up. Quit your bellyaching."

Maccoby thinks that fathers try to toughen up their sons—even when they're just toddlers—in the hopes of sparing them from the derision and bullying that the fathers know from personal experience will plague them if they appear weak at age 5. She's not suggesting that fathers are heartless. They're parents, after all. They comfort their sons when they're scared, bandage their knees when they're hurt, and so forth. But Maccoby sees fathers playing a dual role: being nurturing, on the one hand, and "participating in the induction of boys into male peer culture," on the other hand. As part of that induction, fathers teach their sons to avoid acting like girls.

Of course, fathers' indoctrination both prepares sons for the demands of the playground and perpetuates the legacy of those demands. By the time boys start kindergarten, they don't need their fathers to tell them to act tough. Many have learned this lesson so well that they teach it to the boys who haven't yet got it right (and who may well have fathers who tried to break the legacy). They make fun of boys who talk to girls or enjoy feminine activities or just don't seem tough enough. At summer camp when David was 6, one of the tests of toughness devised by the boys in his group was to cross the monkey bars of an old metal jungle gym. The peeling paint on the metal bars made the feat especially difficult because the bars scraped the children's hands. David's hands were blistered and bloody from the effort, but he proved himself. The physical pain may well have been less severe than the psychological pain he'd have had if the other boys thought he had wimped out.

What about girls? They're not as strongly sex typed as boys are because they don't feel as much pressure from their parents or from one another to be feminine as boys do to be masculine. Because traditionally male activities have more status than traditionally female activities, girls who don't conform to gender stereotypes are seen as smart, spirited, and liberated. Take sports, for instance. More girls are involved in organized sports today than at any other time in U.S. history. And female athletes are cool, whether they are professionals in the National Women's Basketball League or the United States women's soccer team or local sports heroes at school. "My daughter loves football and knows a lot about it" said Shari, of her 8 year old. She said that watching games on TV is a bonding experience for father and daughter. None of her daughter's girlfriends have any interest in football, and her daughter regrets not being able to talk about it with them. But they don't tease her for her interest in the sport.

Though girls feel freer to tread on traditionally male territory than boys do on female territory, most girls still prefer playing with girls, at least until around age 11. They want to be accepted by other girls and will do what it takes to show that they're one of the group, which often means playing in a traditionally feminine way. Six-year-old Emma loves karate and basketball and hates Barbies. She doesn't try to hide her love of sports (that's cool), but she told her mother that she pretends to like Barbies when she's with other girls so that they'll like her.

BOYS AND GIRLS TOGETHER

Of course, boys and girls don't avoid each other entirely from the day they enter preschool until the night they attend their first dance. In public and in coed private schools, boys and girls have no choice but to sit side by side in classrooms and work together on school projects. They're grouped by ability into the same reading groups, gifted programs, and special education classes. Common interests draw them together in after-school activities like soccer, group music lessons, and school plays. And girls and boys with common interests and experiences develop a sense of camaraderie. On the last day of the second grade, my son came off the bus bursting with pride because a girl from his preschool class had won the art award for their grade. The two hadn't played together or even been in the same class in four years, yet David still felt a bond with her.

Alliances between boys and girls are less likely to deepen into friendships than alliances between two children of the same sex. But boy-girl friendships do develop, and they develop more often than social scientists have long assumed. It's so common for elementary school boys to play only with boys and girls with girls that for a long time psychologists thought that those who didn't follow the pattern were abnormal—social outcasts who had trouble getting along with children of their own sex. But, on the contrary, it now seems that most of the children in boy-girl friendships are not only well adjusted but may be among the smartest and most popular children in their classes.

In a 1995 study, psychologists at the University of Michigan interviewed 723 third and fourth graders, asking them to name their best friends and the most popular classmates. Only 92 children, or 14 percent of the total, had at least one friend of the other sex, but most of those who did also had plenty of friends of their own sex. In fact, they were among the best-liked children, as judged by their classmates, and among the strongest academically, as judged by their teachers. The researchers concluded that the children who were able to be friends with both boys and girls were the social and academic leaders.

What the study didn't ask was whether these boy-girl friends hung out much together at school or whether they saw each other mainly outside school. Boys and girls are more inclined to play together outside school than at school during recess or lunch. In *Gender Play*, Barrie Thorne describes the following encounter between Melanie, a sixth grader, and a classmate named Jack on their elementary school playground. After Jack walked by without even glancing at Melanie, she whispered to Thorne, "He's one of my best friends."

"But you didn't even nod or say hello to each other," Thorne said.

"We're friends in our neighborhood and at church," Melanie replied, "but at school we pretend not to know each other so we won't get teased."

Thorne thinks that there are two reasons why children are more likely to be teased in school for playing with children of the other sex than for doing the same thing outside school. One is that there are more children to choose from at school, which means there's less reason not to play with classmates of the same sex. Second, school lunchrooms and playgrounds are highly public places where it's impossible to escape the scrutiny and judgment of one's peers. In an environment where there are groups of girls here and groups of boys there, a kind of group-think prevails, with children getting swept up in an us-versus-them mindset.

Back home, away from the madding crowd, children have fewer choices of playmates but more freedom of choice. When David was in kindergarten, he said that he couldn't play with girls at school because the boys would make fun of him. But when he came home, he often played with the two girls his age on our block. They'd play board games or go on the backyard swings. They had a great time, and David didn't have to take any flack from the guys. Many of "the guys" also waved the rule when they were on their home turf. One day David was playing at the home of a boy when a girl from their class who lived around the corner invited them over to her backyard swimming pool. They gladly went and had a wonderful time, free of social stigma.

Should parents and teachers try to get boys and girls to play together? Cross-sex friendships may have advantages, such as promoting greater understanding and cooperation and less stereotyped attitudes. But fighting nature isn't easy. Maccoby and other researchers have found that when individual teachers make boys and girls play together in school for a limited time as an experiment, the effort works, but only until the teacher stops enforcing cross-sex play. Afterward, the boys go right back to playing mainly with other boys and the girls with other girls. Not only that, but the children often grumble about the exercise and resent the teacher for forcing them to go through with it.

Even so, adults can set up situations that make boys and girls want to play together. What has been shown to make a difference is a preschool or an elementary school with a strong and clear philosophy of gender equity. In one study, researchers compared the amount of boy-girl play at two preschools: a traditional one and a progressive one in which teachers tried harder to avoid gender stereotypes and bias. The children at each school were in the same age range (4 to 6 years old) and were equally social, spending about 80 percent of their time playing with other children. But the children at the traditional school spent 70 percent of their playtime with same-sex playmates, whereas the children at the progressive school spent just 41 percent of their time this way. Thorne found a similar difference in comparing children in progressive and traditional elementary schools.

KISSY GIRLS, KISSY BOYS, AND SEXUAL HARASSMENT

Alice and Peter, 4¹/₂-year-old classmates, have regular play dates, which Alice calls "dates." Sitting together at the library for a preschool story hour one afternoon, Peter slipped his arm around Alice's shoulders, evoking titters from the mothers and nannies behind them.

Four-year-old Tyler told his father that there were two girls in his class whom he wanted to marry. In a lighthearted way, his father explained that he couldn't marry both girls because that was illegal in this country. The boy came up with a creative solution to the problem. He said that he and the girls would move to a country where having more than one wife was legal.

One of the paradoxes of children's social lives is that during the years when many girls play only with girls and boys play only with boys, many children also develop their first crush. Tyler's father was amused by his son's crush. As far as he was concerned, it was innocent and harmless and entirely normal. Experts agree. They look upon children's crushes as an extension of their love for their families. Estelle Zarowin, a clinical social worker at the Child Development Center of the Jewish Board of Family and Children's Services in New York, sees crushes as a reassuring sign. "Take pride in your child's ability to express affection," she told *Parents* magazine. "It means you've raised a loving, secure child." For girls, Zarowin said, crushes may have the added dimension of romantic fantasy play of the sort that is certainly more common among girls than boys. "Having a crush may make girls feel more grown-up."

Talk about who's marrying whom may be normal and cute, but when crushes involve kissing, adults hear alarm bells. Several of the parents in my son's kindergarten class complained to the teacher when their children came home with stories about kissing. There were "kissy girls," who went around kissing boys, and "kissy boys," who went around kissing girls. As my son told it, kissy girls were to be avoided. Being kissed by one was a social stigma for a boy. But being a kissy boy or being called one was even worse. In response to the parents' complaints, the teacher had "a little talk about germs" with the class, and then the kissing stopped.

Not all children get off so easily. In a world that has become sensitive to unwanted advances, some young children who kiss and hug their classmates have recently been accused of sexual harassment. A 6-year-old boy in North Carolina was suspended from his elementary school in 1996 after he kissed a girl on the cheek. This incident made headlines around the country, and several schools have since passed rules against touching—hugging and hand-holding included.

For all the attention it gets, kissing is pretty rare among young children. The largest survey of sexual behavior in young children found that only 8 percent of 2- to 5-year-old boys and 7 percent of girls in this age group kiss other children sometimes and that the incidence declines until age 12. Many adults assume that there's some early sexual feeling behind this kind of behavior, but therapists say that there isn't, at least not in preschoolers and early elementary school students. When young children try to kiss other children their age, it's usually because they want to make friends and don't know a more socially acceptable way to do it.

However, the stirrings of true sexual attraction may begin earlier than most parents expect it to—soon after a child turns 9, according to a new theory. This is the age when both boys and girls have a surge in dehydroepiandrosterone, or DHEA, a sex hormone released by the adrenal glands. DHEA is popularly known as an antiaging supplement, although its function as a fountain of youth has not been proved. But DHEA is known to stimulate physical changes in children. For one thing, it causes the oil-producing sebaceous glands in the skin to develop and also seems to cause a growth spurt. The new theory is that it ignites the spark of sexual attraction, too.

That's a radical notion about children in middle childhood, the years from roughly 5 to 10, when children have been seen as decidedly asexual. But the theory comes from two scientists at the University of Chicago, Martha McClintock, a biopsychologist and MacArthur Foundation fellow, and Gilbert Herdt, an anthropologist who specializes in the development of sexual identity. McClintock and Herdt base their idea on the results of three studies in which adults were asked to recall how old they were the first time they felt sexually attracted to someone. The mean age was between 9 and 10. Since DHEA levels increase sharply after age 9, the researchers think that it helps promote the first sexual feelings.

SEXUAL BEHAVIOR IN YOUNG CHILDREN

Many parents have received or made phone calls that go something like this: "Your son [or daughter] pulled down his [or her] pants in front of my daughter [or son]." For decades, child care authorities like Benjamin Spock reassured parents that occasional exhibitionism is normal in young children. The same goes for masturbation. But in recent years, it's become clear that engaging in certain sexual behavior often indicates that a child has been sexually abused. And since all states and the District of Columbia require teachers, physicians, and other people who work with children to report cases of suspected child abuse to local child protective services agencies, phones ring when a child is seen peeking at another child's genitals or regularly touching his or her own private parts.

William Friedrich, a psychologist at the Mayo Clinic, often counsels such children. He recalled a third-grade girl whose teacher suspected sexual abuse because she had a habit of putting her hands between her legs as she sat in class. But after talking with the girl, Friedrich could see that her behavior stemmed not from sexual abuse but from a childish lack of self-control. She simply needed a gentle reminder of where *not* to put her hands in public. Like Friedrich, divorce lawyers are also consulted when a child behaves in a sexual way. They get frantic calls from parents accusing their ex-husbands and ex-wives' new partners of sexually abusing their children if, for example, the children are caught with a playmate saying something like, "I'll show you mine if you show me yours."

Parents and teachers aren't the only ones who get confused about what sort of sexual behavior is normal. In this climate of suspicion, even the professionals who are consulted, like psychologists and pediatricians, are sometimes unsure, since until recently there was little research. Friedrich set out to find some answers, and in 1998 he and his colleagues published the largest, most comprehensive study of sexual behavior in children.

They interviewed the mothers of 1,114 children from ages 2 to 12 in Minnesota and Los Angeles, asking how often their children displayed each of thirty-eight kinds of sexual behavior in the previous six months. The behaviors included masturbation, showing their genitals to adults, and trying to see or touch other people's genitals. The researchers excluded children from the study if they showed signs of having been sexually abused, on the basis of their responses to psychological screenings. So, whichever kinds of sexual behavior were reported for a large share of the children—in this case, 20 percent or more—were considered normal.

Sexual behavior was most prevalent among the youngest children, the 2- to 5 year olds. The most common behaviors were touching their own genitals at home, touching their mothers' or other women's breasts, and trying to see other people naked or undressing. Most of these behaviors were equally common among boys and girls. The exception was touching their own genitals, which was much more common in boys. Sixty percent of the boys and about 44 percent of the girls were seen doing so at home in the previous six months. Forty-two percent of the girls and 43 percent of the boys tried to touch women's breasts, and 26 percent of the boys and girls tried to peak at people when they were naked or undressing.

The mothers saw less sexual behavior in the older children, which wasn't surprising since after about age 5, children become more modest. Only two kinds of sexual behavior were prevalent enough to be considered normal in the 6 to 9 year olds: touching their own genitals (reported for about 40 percent of the boys and 21 percent of the girls) and peeking at people who were undressing or nude (20 percent of the boys and girls). The only sexual behavior that the 10- to 12 year olds revealed to their mothers was interest in the other sex. No surprise there.

Other sorts of sexual displays were relatively rare in children of all ages, including touching other children's genitals, making sexual sounds, kissing other children, and kissing adults they didn't know well. This isn't to say that you should jump to conclusions if your child does one of these things once or twice, Friedrich said. Just tell your child to stop. If the behavior ends, chances are there's nothing to worry about. But if it persists, it could be a sign of sexual abuse or exposure to other forms of violence. By the same token, he said, even one of the normal behaviors may indicate one of these problems in a child who engages in it often or compulsively.

This survey didn't help answer another nagging question about sexual behavior in children: Where is the line between "normal" boy-girl teasing and sexual harassment. But in a landmark decision in 1999, the Supreme Court helped draw that line. The

Court heard the case of a fifth-grade girl in Georgia who for months had been subject to teasing, poking, and grabbing by a boy who sat next to her in class. The girl's mother complained to the teachers and school administrators, but they did nothing to stop the boy. The girl's teacher wouldn't even move the boy's and the girl's desks apart. Eventually, the girl's mother went to the police. The boy pleaded guilty to charges of sexual battery and was convicted of the offense in juvenile court. But because the school authorities didn't try to stop the boy, the girl's mother sued the board of education of her daughter's school district for violating Title IX of the Education Amendments of 1972, the federal law that bars sexual discrimination at school.

The Court ruled that schools can be held liable for doing nothing to stop one student from sexually harassing another. The majority opinion described sexual harassment as behavior "so severe, pervasive and objectively offensive that it denies its victims the equal access to education" guaranteed by Title IX. But "simple acts of teasing and name-calling among schoolchildren" are not sexual harassment, the majority opinion said.

Although the difference between teasing and sexual harassment is sure to be debated for years, the Supreme Court decision put into sharper focus the boundaries of acceptable behavior in boys and girls. On the day the decision was handed down, a lawyer for the National Association of Secondary School Principals told the *New York Times*, "The days of boys will be boys and girls will be girls are long gone."

CHILDREN WHO DON'T FIT THE MOLD

Five-year-old Jack doesn't enjoy sports or other rough play, and he steers clear of boys who do. Instead of playing tee ball and soccer, he signed up for an after-school cooking class. On the playground at recess, he's often by himself or talking with one of the teacher's aides about his far-flung interests, which include geology and ancient Egypt, subjects that children his age don't know much about. Yet Jack isn't a social outcast. He's regularly invited to birthday parties and asked for play dates. His friends are other quiet, thoughtful boys.

At a time when most children are walking, breathing gender stereotypes, many children seem oblivious to them or openly defy them. Everyone knows boys who are subdued and sensitive and would rather, say, go to an art museum than a football game. Everyone knows girls who are natural athletes, who don't wear dresses and spend more time getting their nails dirty than getting them painted. There's a bit of yin and yang in each child. To his world in suburban Boston, 7-year-old Nathaniel projects the image of a jock. But in the privacy of his home, he loves to dance with his mom. A Buffalo mother said that her teenage son's favorite color is pink, and though he doesn't advertise this preference to his classmates, he has no problem wearing pink clothes to school. The mothers of these boys applaud their individualism.

In years past, the idea of a boy wearing pink or, for that matter, a girl showing more interest in a career than in marriage was considered unorthodox. In *Man and Woman, Boy and Girl*, a classic work on gender identity originally published in 1973, interest in a career was one of the characteristics that was said to distinguish female hermaphrodites from normal girls. "When queried about the priority of a nondomestic career versus marriage and being a housewife in the future," the book states, "the majority of fetally androgenized girls subordinated marriage to career, or else wanted an occupational career other than housewife concurrent with being married, and regarded occupational and marital status as equally important."

Such notions about what constitutes normal and abnormal gender behavior are outdated now. But even though the line separating normal from abnormal has moved, people disagree over where it belongs. And in the absence of firm rules, even parents who raise their children to be free of conventional gender stereotypes admit to feeling uneasy when their children deviate too far from them, whatever "too far" means.

Karen came home one day to find her 4-year-old son wearing nail polish. It seems that the au pair had painted Karen's daughter's nails and then Karen's son asked to have his nails done. Karen, who considers herself a progressive thinker, was surprised by how much the site of her son in nail polish disturbed her. She told the au pair never to do that again.

Like Karen, my husband and I faced the limits of our tolerance for gender-atypical behavior when Sarah, at age 5, announced that she wanted to have her hair cut short so she would "look like a boy." We didn't directly refuse, for fear of ratcheting up her determination to have a bob. But we kept telling her how beautiful her long hair was. When I took her for a haircut, I knew Sarah wouldn't be satisfied with just a trim, so I told the stylist to cut several inches off, bringing her hair to shoulder length. We were all happy.

A lot of young children occasionally fantasize about being the other sex. About 14 percent of 2- to 5-year-old boys sometimes dress up like girls, according to Friedrich's survey of sexual behavior in children. And about 6 percent of boys in this age range say that they want to be girls. By the same token, 8 percent of girls that age say that they want to be boys. The survey shows that these behaviors decline with age. Only 6 percent of the 6- to 9-year-old boys ever dress like girls and 4 percent wish to be girls, and just 3.5 percent of the girls this age wish to be boys. What the findings suggest is that young children try out a range of cross-gender behaviors, but that as they get older and develop a firmer sense of their gender identity, their desire to experiment wanes. What the survey doesn't say is which cross-gender behaviors are normal and which ones aren't. But behavioral scientists are trying to come up with answers.

GENDER IDENTITY DISORDER

Ludovic's family had just moved into a suburban neighborhood and invited all the families on the block to a party. The guests were socializing in the backyard, and the party was going well until 7-year-old Ludovic appeared. He was wearing his sister's dress, shoes, earrings, and lipstick. All the guests stopped talking and stared. Ludovic's father tried to pass off his son's appearance as a joke, but as the days passed, it was clear that Ludovic wasn't joking. He brought a doll to school, and the children made fun of him. At recess, no one would play with him. He managed to make friends with the boy across the street, but one day when they were playing at his house, the boy's mother walked in on Ludovic dressed in her daughter's clothing and pretending to marry her son. She forbade her son from playing with Ludovic again.

Ludovic believed he was really a girl. As proof, he told his mother that he had stomach cramps, which he took as a sign that he was about to begin menstruating. Ludovic's parents then took Ludovic to a psychologist, but he didn't change. Meanwhile, Ludovic's behavior made everyone who knew him and his family so uneasy that the family became outcasts: The boy was kicked out of school, and his father was fired from his job. The family relocated in the hopes of starting a new life.

Ludovic is the main character in *Ma Vie en Rose*, a 1996 Belgian film, but there are real children like him. They are said to have gender identity disorder, a psychiatric condition in which a boy has a female gender identity and a girl has a male gender identity. Gender identity disorder doesn't apply to boys just because they sometimes go to the dress-up area at school or try on their mother's lipstick and high heels. Nor does it apply to girls who prefer climbing trees to playing with dolls, who want to be Batman for Halloween, or who occasionally say that they wish they could be boys because boys have more fun.

Children with gender identity disorder don't merely pretend they are someone of the other sex; they persistently long to be the other sex or insist that they are. The American Psychiatric Association's diagnostic manual outlines two broad categories of behavior that are signs of gender identity disorder in a child: acting like the other sex and showing discomfort with his or her own sex. These behaviors must be repeated, persistent, and intense. A child is seen as acting like the other sex if he or she does four of these five things: says that he or she wants to be the other sex, cross-dresses, pretends to be the other sex while playing, prefers toys and activities that are associated with the other sex, and prefers playing with children of the other sex. A child is seen as being uncomfortable with his or her own sex if the child shows a strong aversion toward activities and clothing associated with that sex and a dislike of his or her anatomy. For example, a boy may say that he hates his penis or wishes that he didn't have one. A girl may deny that she will grow breasts when she gets older. Again, these behaviors must be strong and persist for at least six months to be considered abnormal.

Of the children who are evaluated by doctors for gender identity disorder, boys outnumber girls by 7 to 1, according to Susan Bradley and Kenneth Zucker, leading experts on the condition who are with the Child and Adolescent Gender Identity Clinic at the Clarke Institute of Psychiatry in Toronto. But these numbers don't necessarily mean that the disorder is really so much more common in boys. Bradley and Zucker say that the numbers may reflect society's lower tolerance for feminine behavior in boys than for masculine behavior in girls.

Like many other psychiatric conditions in children, gender identity disorder was long blamed on parents. Professionals no longer believe that parents are the cause, but they do think that trouble at home contributes to the problem. Many children with gender identity disorder have parents who suffer from depression. And many of the girls have been sexually abused by their fathers.

But most children with depressed or abusive parents don't develop gender identity disorder, so experts think that those who do are born with a biological predisposition to it. The theory is that girls with the disorder were exposed to too much androgen in the womb and boys with the disorder were exposed to too little and that these abnormal hormone levels affected the children's brain development, the source of their gender identity.

HOMOSEXUALITY

No one knows what makes people gay or straight. And it's impossible to predict a child's sexual orientation on the basis of his or her behavior at age 4, 6, or 8. But unsettling as it seems, it's hard to ignore the scientific evidence that sexual orientation, or at least an inclination toward one, forms around the same time as gender identity in early childhood. Research suggests that one of the strongest indicators of sexual orientation for males, at least, is how boys play. In other words, boys who have few or no male playmates and who don't enjoy conventionally masculine activities and play styles are likely to grow up to be gay.

Just how likely? In a landmark study, Richard Green, a psychologist at the University of California at Los Angeles, compared 66 boys who played and acted in effeminate ways at age 7 with a control group of 56 boys who showed no feminine traits to see how many ended up being gay or straight. Green was able to follow two-thirds of these boys until they were teenagers or young adults. He found that 75 percent of boys who exhibited effeminate behavior at age 7 said that they had mainly homosexual or bisexual fantasies by the time they were, on average, age 19. And 80 percent of those who'd had sex were bisexual or homosexual. In contrast, fewer than 4 percent of the control group became homosexual or bisexual.

Not all homosexuals had gender identity problems as children. A meta-analysis of other studies in which homosexual men and women recalled their behavior as children found that only about half the homosexual men enjoyed cross-gender play and other behavior as boys. The relationship between childhood behavior and women's sexual orientation was even weaker.

Still, the fact that there's a link at all between childhood play and adult sexual orientation raises the question of whether homosexuality is biological or possibly genetic. Homosexuality does seem to run in families. A study of gay men with twin brothers found that 52 percent of the identical twins were also gay, whereas just 22 percent of the fraternal twins were. A study of lesbian women and their twin sisters found similar results. Identical twins have identical genes, whereas fraternal twins don't. So, if there were a "gay gene," all the identical twins in the study would share it. The fact that all the identical twins weren't gay or straight doesn't disprove the notion of a genetic underpinning of homosexuality, but it suggests that the gene—if it exists—doesn't automatically make all people who inherit it gay. Other factors must come into play.

Several years ago, headlines trumpeted the strongest evidence yet that homosexuality was inherited. A study in the journal *Science* in 1993 looked at the X (female) chromosome of 40 pairs of homosexual brothers and found that 33 of the pairs had a marker on a small part of the chromosome. Some scientists wondered if the marker was, or pointed the way to, the elusive gay gene. But since then, other researchers have been unable to find the marker in most of the gay men studied, so the notion that homosexuality is genetic remains controversial.

At about the same time that some scientists were looking for signs of homosexuality in the genes, others were looking for signs in the brain. Simon LeVay, a neuroscientist, found that one speck of the hypothalamus, called the third interstitial nuclei of the anterior hypothalamus, had fewer neurons in homosexual men than in heterosexuals. The INAH-3 is also smaller in women than in men (see Chapter 1, page 8). The study got a lot of publicity after it was published in 1991, and the finding was taken to mean that homosexuality was hardwired in the brain. But, as with the genetic research, other scientists haven't found the same difference in the brains of homosexuals and heterosexuals.

Despite all the unanswered questions about what determines a person's sexual orientation, experts agree on at least one point: There's nothing that parents or therapists can or should do to change it. In recent years, many professional health organizations have condemned the long-standing practice of using psychotherapy or other interventions to "treat" homosexuality. For one thing, these groups affirm that homosexuality isn't a mental illness and therefore is not something that needs therapy. In addition, attempts to change a person's sexual orientation don't achieve their goal, but they can cause depression, anxiety, and self-destructive behavior.

However, individual or family therapy can be helpful for some children whose gender identity is at odds with their sex. For one thing, it can help diagnose and treat other psychiatric problems that are common in such children, including depression. Family therapy can help identify and treat the problems that are common among the parents of such children, including depression, substance abuse, and family violence. Therapy can also help the children socially. Children whose behavior is atypical for their sex are often bullied by other children. So, therapists work on strategies that the children can use to prevent or stand up to the bullying and to make friends. One such strategy is to suggest that the children reduce their cross-gender behavior at school.

For many families, the most important goal of therapy is to help parents overcome their disappointment that their child is not as they expected him or her to be. Dr. Barbara Staggers, director of adolescent medicine at Children's Hospital Oakland in Oakland, California, who counsels teenagers with gender identity issues, said that the process is akin to grieving in that parents must cope with the "loss" of their idealized child. Like all children, those with gender identity disorder or homosexual tendencies need their parents' love and support. Love and support can't change their gender identity or sexual orientation, but they can make a difference between whether the children are tormented by their feelings or at peace with them.

SUMMING UP

People who come to parenting with the ideal of raising a gender-neutral child are in for disappointment. Children aren't gender neutral. Nearly all children go through a stage when they look and act more like stereotypes of girls and boys than like individuals, even children who are raised in households where Dad cooks and cleans and Mom is the main breadwinner.

Gender-typed behavior starts to become especially pronounced at about ages 3 or 4, after children have reached the developmental milestone of gender identity and can correctly and consistently say, "I am a boy" or "I am a girl." Young girls to try hard to play the girl role and young boys try hard to play the boy role. Of course, they are encouraged to do so at every turn by TV commercials; playmates who are nicer to them when they play in gender-appropriate ways; and parents who, often without realizing it, have subtle ways of rewarding masculine play for boys and feminine play for girls.

As with the preference for dolls or guns, most children seek out same-sex playmates as they follow the learning curve of gender identity. Many researchers think that girls play mainly with girls and boys with boys because they have fundamentally different play styles, with boys being rougher and wilder and girls being more nurturing. The same differences are seen among primates. Male monkeys play-fight and congregate mainly with other male monkeys. Female monkeys groom one another and play mainly with other female monkeys. In primates as well as humans, the different play styles are probably related partially to sex differences in the brain that have been shaped by exposure to different levels of sex hormones before birth. But among humans, the degree of separation is also influenced by social factors— it's greatest in the most sexist societies.

Child's play isn't just about fighting and grooming, guns and dolls. Scientists are revising the long-held view of middle childhood—the elementary school years—as being emphatically asexual. On the contrary, the first signs of sexual attraction may appear as early as the third grade. Even younger children exhibit sexual behavior, like kissing a classmate or peeking at each other's genitals. Scientists are only beginning to study such behaviors in young children and answer the question that parents have asked all along: Which ones are normal? At the same time, the courts are beginning to sort out which kinds of sexual behaviors in children are "legal" and which ones constitute sexual harassment at school.

SUGGESTIONS FOR PARENTS

Conforming to gender stereotypes may be a normal part of growing up, but it can also restrict a child's opportunities for learning and development. The challenge for parents is to recognize when stereotypical behavior is benign and when it is potentially harmful. Here are some guidelines.

Don't Sweat over Toys. In a perfect world, your children would spend all their time playing with only educational, gender-neutral toys like puzzles and board games. But in reality they don't. Girls also like dolls and tutus. Boys like trucks and action figures. Fortunately, research hasn't found that children who play with sex-typed toys go on to become more sex typed or less intelligent than other children. Many of the toys favored by boys, like Legos, are seen as desirable because they help develop skills like spatial sense and hand-eye coordination. But many traditionally feminine toys, like stringing beads, develop these skills, too, only they don't get as much credit. The bottom line: Give your children a good mix of toys and then let them play with whichever ones they like. Toys aren't worth a battle.

Talk About Sexism. No matter how hard you try to avoid giving gender labels to toys and activities, your children are still bound to encounter sexist attitudes. An uncle may tell your son, "Boys don't cry," or a grandparent may chide your daughter for not being "ladylike" when she hangs upside down from the monkey bars. You don't want to play gender cop, exposing each and every gender-bias infraction and, in the process, risk boring or annoying your children. But, at the same time, you don't want your impressionable child to be influenced by prejudice.

Carol Nagy Jacklin struggled with this dilemma as a parent. Looking back, she wishes that she'd given her children fewer lectures on sexism and more tools for recognizing it. As she sees it, the best tools are words that give gender bias a stigma. "Words have power," Jacklin said. The term *sexual harassment* has raised our awareness of the problem of boys groping and sexually taunting girls in school to the point that the Supreme Court declared such behavior illegal. Jacklin thinks that families should devise phrases for types of gender bias that don't yet have labels—things like giving girls' athletics short shrift and teasing boys who show emotion.

Practice What You Preach. If you want your children to grow up to question gender stereotypes, don't perpetuate them at home. In two-parent households, that means that mom and dad should cook and do housework and share in important decision making. Being models of gender equity may not prevent your 3 or 4 year old from picking up gender-typed behavior as a means of understanding his or her gender identity, but it will increase the odds that the child will outgrow them. As children's sense of themselves comes together, stereotypical behavior tends to fall apart or, at least, to coexist with broader pursuits. A girl can love nail polish as well as astronomy. And a boy can blow away the enemy on the computer screen and then log off and play the piano. So be patient.

4

Boys and Girls in School

Myths About Gender and Aptitude

KEEPING SCORE

The mothers of two second-grade boys were standing outside the classroom one morning looking at writing samples from each of the children about a book they'd read. One of the mothers shook her head. "This kid wrote two pages. My son wrote three sentences," she said.

"My son didn't write much either," said the other mother. Then she looked at the two-page sample. "What do you expect? It was written by a girl."

On another day, the mother of a girl in the class was lamenting her daughter's difficulty with multiplication. The mother thought that her daughter's struggle was gender related. As evidence, she pointed to herself. "I was really bad in math," she said.

Parents chatting in school hallways aren't the only ones who wonder, however reluctantly, whether a child's strength in different academic subjects has anything to do with his or her sex. Scientists do, too. That's because there are sex differences in standardized test scores. Girls do better on standardized reading and writing tests. Boys do better on standardized math tests.

The achievement gaps have narrowed in recent years as gender bias in the classroom has diminished. But because the gaps haven't disappeared, neither have the age-old questions about sex, aptitude, and intelligence: Are boys fundamentally better at math than girls? Are girls better readers and writers? Is there a gender difference in IQ? Some scientists say that the persistent sex differences in intellectual performance are the handiwork of sex hormones shaping the brain. Other scientists say that it's impossible to draw that conclusion without first eliminating gender bias in education.

These questions are every bit as political as they are scientific. No area of gender difference is more polemical than the nature versus nurture of intelligence and achievement. But this chapter moves beyond politics. It lays out the possible biological and social reasons why gender differences in performance persist. More important, it points up why biological evidence doesn't justify the old-style tendency among teachers and parents to funnel boys and girls toward some subjects and activities and away from others. To the contrary, many researchers now say that the only way to achieve gender equity in education is to understand whether there really are biological reasons for the gender gaps. If boys and girls do learn some subjects more easily than others, understanding how and why is the first step toward adjusting teaching methods to help them learn more effectively.

GENERAL INTELLIGENCE: DOES SEX MATTER?

General intelligence, measured by IQ tests, is the ability to learn new skills and juggle several tasks and changing situations. It's considered a good predictor of how well a child will do in school and how many years the child will stay in school, as well as how successful he or she will be as an adult on the job. Genetics plays a big role, with a child's general IQ estimated to be 30 percent to 50 percent inherited. Much of the remaining 50 percent to 70 percent is shaped by experience—the quality of the child's everyday life as indicated by things like ready access to educational toys and books, trips to museums and plays, good schools, and loving parents. What has long been debated is what, if any, role sex plays in a person's IQ.

For years it was a given that males were more intelligent than females. After all, they needed the extra smarts to go to college, run companies, become physicians, and do all sorts of things that, with rare exceptions, only males did. But about a century ago, when scientists tried to prove scientifically that males were smarter, they were in for a surprise. Many of the studies showed either no differences or only minor ones, and when there were differences, they were in females' favor. The mainly male scientists didn't know what to make of the findings, so they dismissed them.

Helen Thompson Woolley, a psychologist at Columbia University, marveled at her colleagues' reluctance to pay attention to tests showing that girls were smarter than boys. "So far as I know, no one has drawn the conclusion that girls have greater native ability than boys," she wrote in 1914. "One is tempted to indulge in idle speculation as to whether this admirable restraint from hasty generalization would have been equally marked had the sex findings been reversed!"

Today, there are several different intelligence tests, and boys and girls get about the same overall scores on most of them. There's more variation among the scores of boys as a group and girls as a group than there is between the two groups. But even though their general intelligence is pretty much equal, boys and girls get different scores on the subsets of intelligence measured by IQ tests. Boys do better on most of the questions that have to do with spatial ability. Girls do better on most of the language questions. So nearly a century of intelligence testing has shifted the question from who's smarter to why do boys and girls seem to be smarter in different areas?

SPATIAL ABILITY

The term *spatial ability* covers a lot of territory. It's imagining how an object looks from all sides. It's mentally folding a piece of paper to envision how it could be made into a desired shape, as one might do before starting an origami project. It's detecting patterns in a group of shapes. It's recognizing how objects, like a bat and a ball, are related to each other in a space. It's making mental maps of places and finding your way from point A to point B. It's remembering what objects were left in a given place and where they were. A common denominator of the spatial tasks is that they're nonverbal.

I became especially curious about the superiority of boys' spatial skills when my son got a card game called Set, which may as well be called the spatial relations game. To play, you lay out fifteen cards in a grid. The cards show images that differ by shape, number, color, and shading. The object of the game is to find three cards that share a pattern. The pattern can be the identical image on all three cards. Or it can be three different shapes present in the same quantity, color, and shading. It can also be three different shapes, colorings, and shadings but with the same quantity of shapes.

David was phenomenal at this game. He consistently saw

more patterns and identified them faster than I did. The only time I was able to beat David was when he was so sick with the flu that he could barely lift his head off the couch. Since my husband was also good at the game, I figured that his and David's superior skills might be a male thing.

This is the kind of snap judgment that leads to false generalizations. Needless to say, I was in for a surprise when I looked at scientific studies comparing males' and females' performance on different spatial tasks. Although the studies do show that boys are better on some of them, the Set-type task of finding patterns isn't one of them. It turns out, boys and girls do equally well at this one. There are only two spatial skills at which boys and men are consistently better. One is mentally rotating an object to envision how it looks from different sides. The other is generating a mental map of a place they've visited perhaps once but don't know well, a skill that's useful for finding their way around unfamiliar territory.

Mental rotation is measured by the Mental Rotation Test, a standardized test that asks questions about drawings of three-dimensional objects from different angles. One question shows five shapes that look different from one another and asks which two, when rotated, are identical to the first shape. People must figure out the answer in a limited amount of time. Four out of five boys aged 15 to 20 do better than most of girls in this age range. Since this test is fairly complicated, it's not usually given to younger children, but several studies using simpler tests show that boys as young as 4½ perform better than do girls. One test involves copying a three-dimensional Lego model, and another involves constructing a three-dimensional model of the children's classroom.

Other spatial intelligence tests assess the ability to create mental maps. Researchers first show children a map, then take it away and ask them to draw the map from memory. The researchers evaluate the maps' accuracy based on such things as the clustering of landmarks and the geometric representation of these features—for example, showing the gas station southwest of the post office. For all ages starting at 8, boys create more accurate maps. In his book, *Male/Female*, David Geary, a psychologist at the University of Missouri, described a study in which maps were assigned ranks ranging from Level 1 (disorganized and inaccurate) to Level 3 (highly organized and accurate). To prevent possible gender bias in the study, the researchers had the maps scored by judges who did not know the sex of the children who drew them. The judges gave the top rank to 29 percent of the boys' maps and only 7 percent of the girls' maps. And they gave the bottom rank to 23 percent of the girls' maps and 6 percent of the boys' maps.

Mental rotation and navigation aren't the sorts of skills that are taught in school, so it seems unlikely that boys' strong showing would be due to gender bias favoring them in the classroom. But are these spatial skills hardwired in boys' brains?

Biological Factors

For decades, researchers have assumed that there must be some biological reason why boys consistently outperform girls in mental rotation and navigation. At first, they entertained the possibility of a gene inherited mainly by boys, but a spatial relations gene was never found. Lately, with the advent of brain-imaging technology, the search for the biological roots of spatial ability has shifted to the brain.

Observations of brain activity during spatial tasks show that boys and men are more lateralized, meaning that they use mainly the right hemisphere, and girls and women use both sides of the brain. Although both sides of the brain are involved in spatial reasoning, studies suggest that the right side is more specialized for navigation and mental rotation. Boys rely more heavily on the right hemisphere starting in infancy, so it's possible that they get off to an earlier start connecting up the brain-cell circuits that are important for these spatial tasks.

Navigation and mental rotation also seem to be related to sex hormones. The most vivid evidence comes from experiments involving rats running through mazes, a navigation task. Normally, male meadow voles, a kind of rat, run through mazes better than do females. But in the experiments, female meadow voles that got a shot of testosterone soon after birth ran through the mazes as well as the males. It's possible that testosterone acts on the brain in some way to affect performance on the test.

Some studies also link hormones to spatial skills in humans. Girls with AGS, the condition characterized by exposure to unusually high androgen levels before birth, do much better on the mental rotation test than do other girls. But above a certain level, more androgen doesn't necessarily mean better scores. Men with higher-than-average testosterone levels do worse than other men on the mental rotation test.

Estrogen and progesterone may also affect spatial skills. Some studies show that women's performance on the mental rotation test fluctuates over the course of the menstrual cycle, along with estradiol (a form of estrogen) and progesterone. Most, though not all, of the studies tracking women's performance on the test find that women do best during menstruation, when the levels of estradiol and progesterone are the lowest, and that they do worst in midcycle, when these hormones are the highest. In one study, women's scores were 40 percent to 49 percent higher during menstruation than they were in midcycle.

On the other hand, estrogen and progesterone may enhance

some of the spatial skills that are stronger in girls than in boys. These skills come under the category of visuospatial memory, which involves tasks like remembering where you last saw something. In one study, children aged 8 to 13 were shown a sheet with an array of objects pictured on it. After a minute or so, the sheet was taken away and replaced by two more sheets. The first sheet showed the same objects arranged in the same places as before, as well as a few new objects. The second sheet showed the same items as before, but with some in different places.

The first sheet was a test of straight memory—the children had to circle all objects that were on the original sheet and cross out the new objects. The second sheet tested the children's memory of objects' locations. The children had to circle the objects that were in the same location and cross out those that were moved. The girls of all ages did better than the boys on the straight memory test, but only the adolescent girls did better than the boys on the location memory test. That the girls' superior location memory skill didn't emerge until puberty suggests that sex hormones, which rise during puberty, may affect the brain in some way to give girls an advantage.

Social Factors

If your child's spatial skills were purely the result of biology, he or she wouldn't be able to improve with practice. But your child can improve. People do better on the Mental Rotation Test the second time around. Males still do better than females, but it may well be that they do so because they've had more practice with activities that develop mental rotation ability, like building with blocks and gauging the trajectory of a baseball while standing at home plate. Geary argues that it's not just males' personal experience that has prepared them for mental rotation and navigation, it's the experience of their ancestors. To survive on the hunt for all those years, this line of thinking goes, males needed brains that evolved with a gift for envisioning how an animal looks from different angles (mental rotation) and tracking it down (navigation). How else could men have brought home the buffalo?

You can't change history, but cross-cultural studies bear out the importance of experience for developing spatial skills. In societies where children are kept close to home and have limited opportunities to explore outdoors, boys and girls score relatively low on mental rotation and navigation tests. But in cultures where boys and girls are encouraged to roam and learn their way around, such as in certain Inuit tribes, the children do well on these tests. Although boys still do better, the gender difference isn't as great as it is in cultures where girls are overprotected.

Then again, having the best spatial skills may not have much practical value. Even if girls do have a bit more trouble making maps in their heads, there's no evidence that they have more trouble getting where they need to go. They just use different strategies. Studies show that instead of mentally mapping out an area, girls look for landmarks, like supermarkets and gas stations. In other words, they draw on their visual and spatial memory.

In one set of experiments, Thomas Bever, of the University of Rochester, had some college students test their skill on a computer maze that contained landmarks. When he changed the geometry of the maze but left the landmarks intact, the men's performance suffered. But when he changed or removed the landmarks, the women faltered. What this finding suggests is that males get around by mentally calculating distances between points, whereas females look for familiar buildings and signs. Bever got the same results with male and female rats when had them run around in mazes. When he changed the length of one part of the maze but left the landmarks in, the males got confused and the females found their way around just fine. However, when he took away the landmarks but left the geometry unchanged, the female rats were confused and the male rats were unaffected.

So much for mazes. What about the real world? How relevant are spatial skills to math classes and careers? Common sense tells us that competence in mentally rotating three-dimensional objects is a prerequisite for competence in geometry and for careers like architecture. Studies show that spatial ability and math skills are related—children who are good at one are usually good at the other. And boys as a group do better than girls as a group on standardized math tests.

But above a certain baseline competence, spatial skills don't seem to matter. Carol Beal, of the University of Massachusetts at Amherst, who's been studying girls' math performance, said that training and practice in solving mental rotation problems don't improve children's mathematical performance. The likely reason, she said, is that many mathematical problems can be solved with cognitive skills other than mental rotation, such as verbal and analytical reasoning. Even in careers like architecture that require keen spatial skills, Beal states in her book *Boys and Girls: The Development of Gender Roles*, there is no evidence that those with the best spatial skills are the best in their fields. Given that nearly half of all students in accredited master's degree programs in architecture are women, girls' spatial skills must be good enough.

LANGUAGE ABILITY

Isaac was clearly one of the brightest students in his first-grade class. By the time his teacher introduced the basics of addition and subtraction, Isaac was already multiplying double-digit numbers in his head. He knew dollars and cents so well that when his parents paid for something in a store, he could easily figure out the change they were owed. Isaac's parents would have considered having him skip a grade except for one problem: Isaac was having trouble learning how to read and write. He was in one of the lowest reading groups. And during writing workshop in class, when the students were supposed to sit at their desks and compose short stories or nonfiction, Isaac had trouble thinking of what to say.

Like Isaac, many boys struggle to learn how to read and write. Some scientists and educators think that boys learn to read more slowly than do girls. They don't lag behind girls in all language skills. Boys and girls do equally well on vocabulary tests, including straight word definitions, as well as on tests that require reasoning about words, like making analogies and filling in the missing word in a sentence. They also do equally well on the verbal half of the SAT, the college entrance exam, although its scope is broader than word usage and comprehension. And whatever boys' shortcomings in the language department, they don't keep males from becoming some of the best authors, editors, critics, and linguists.

But when you compare boys as a group with girls as a group, girls' performance in particular language skills is the mirror image of boys' performance on mental rotation and navigation. Girls do significantly better on standardized tests of reading comprehension, grammar, spelling, and writing. The difference appears in elementary school and continues through adulthood.

153

Although talking isn't measured on intelligence tests, girls and women also speak more fluently: They think of the words they want to say more quickly, use more complex sentences, and make fewer grammatical or pronunciation errors.

One reason why boys lag in certain language skills is that they're more prone to some speech and language disabilities. Stuttering is two to four times as common in boys as it is in girls. Reading disabilities are slightly more common in boys, but, what is more significant, boys have a harder time overcoming them. These gender differences suggest that there's something biological, a kind of Achilles heel, that makes many language tasks more difficult for boys than for girls.

Biological Factors

When it comes to language, certain sex differences in the brain may work to females' advantage. Girls' brains develop faster and, in particular, they start using their left hemisphere earlier in infancy. Since the left hemisphere is somewhat more specialized for language than the right hemisphere, its early development may enable girls to start talking earlier than boys. Girls also have more densely packed neurons in areas of the brain that process language: Wernike's area, a commalike section of the left hemisphere, and the posterior temporal cortex. Janet Shucard, a neuroscientist at the State University of New York at Buffalo, thinks that it stands to reason that the extra brain cells devoted to language may give girls an edge in language skills.

There's more. Males' and females' brains operate somewhat differently. When sounding out letters and words, many girls and women use both hemispheres of their brains at once, while nearly all men and boys use just their left hemisphere. Though the left hemisphere seems to do the lion's share of language processing, areas of the right hemisphere work on language, too. So tapping into as many language areas as possible may be an asset.

It remains to be seen whether the female pattern really is better—in other words, if it is why girls and women do better at reading and writing. But the female pattern does seem to be better in one respect: It protects women from language disabilities related to brain damage. Women whose speech is impaired by a stroke have an easier time regaining speech than do men who have the same damage. The likely reason is that women use more of their brain for language, so if one part is harmed, they can compensate by drawing on other parts. Girls may well have a similar advantage with regard to language skills should they suffer some brain damage from an illness or accident.

Social Factors

There's more to a child's success with reading and writing than the circuitry of the brain or the size of the language centers. Like spatial skills, language skills improve with practice. Far more than a child's sex, the experience of being read to from infancy onward gives a child an advantage in learning how to read and write, according to G. Reid Lyon, director of research on learning disabilities at the National Institute of Child and Human Development, a branch of NIH. By looking at books as they're being read aloud, children practice identifying letters and linking them with their sounds. And once they've learned the mechanics of reading, the more that children read, the better they get at it.

Although there's no reason to believe that parents read more to their daughters than to their sons, girls do have other experiences that may enhance their reading and writing abilities.

Parents talk more to their daughters than to their sons from the time they're infants, so girls have more practice with words. But what seems more important than the sheer volume of words is the nature of the conversation.

In particular, girls have more practice using words to describe emotions and relationships. Mothers talk more about feelings to their daughters than to their sons, and girls' friendships are more focused on sharing intimacies. David Geary thinks that girls' proficiency in decoding emotions and probing human relationships enhances girls' understanding of fiction, drama, and poetry, the very kinds of texts for which the gender difference in reading comprehension is the greatest. Geary notes that 7 out of 10 girls and women do better than the average boy and man in reading comprehension of fiction. In contrast, he said, the smallest gender difference in reading comprehension is of nonfiction texts conveying straight information—books on science or urban planning, for instance.

Being cued into the nuances of relationships and feelings may also explain why girls do well in writing. Writing is an emotional experience. Emotions give life to fictitious characters, but even when composing nonfiction—for instance, a short essay for the teacher about a book that was read in class— writers draw on their feelings about the subject and their insights into the characters.

While girls have experiences that support their effort to read and write, boys have experiences that discourage it. Research shows that many parents and teachers think that boys have less basic aptitude for reading and writing than do girls. Parents who hold this view think their sons' language skills are lower than they really are based on tests. Boys pick up on their parents' attitude and then come to think of themselves as poor readers and writers, according to research by Jacquelynne Eccles, a psychologist at the

University of Michigan in Ann Arbor who studies gender differences in education. Children who think they're bad readers don't like reading and, for that reason, they don't read as much as other children. So they have less of a chance of improving. Could we pull up boys' reading and writing scores by giving boys same level of encouragement and experiences delving into emotions and relationships that we give to girls? Maybe. No one's tried to answer the question scientifically. But until someone does, it's impossible to say that a fundamental, biological gender difference in language ability—if it exists—is enough to matter.

GENDER GAPS AT SCHOOL

Back in the old days, teachers, parents, and other adults thought nothing of telling children flat out which classes and extracurricular activities were for boys and which ones were for girls. Boys were encouraged to take physics, calculus, and computer classes, and girls were encouraged to take "softer" classes like art and creative writing. Boys were athletes, girls were cheerleaders. Sex discrimination at school was a fact of life.

Congress officially banned sex discrimination at school in 1972 with Title IX of the Education Amendments. Since then, schools have had to give girls opportunities to play competitive sports, and girls now make up about 40 percent of high school athletes. Schools could no longer open certain courses only to boys and others only to girls. Thanks to Title IX, the notion that shop was for boys and home economics was for girls is as quaint to today's children as the boys' doors and girls' doors at old school buildings. Before Title IX, girls were largely absent from elective math and science classes, but they now take math and science in almost equal numbers as boys.

But gender gaps remain. Although blatant discrimination is rare, research shows that schools still have different expectations for boys and girls in particular subjects and extracurricular activities. And low expectations become self-fulfilling prophecies.

MATH ABILITY: THE WHOLE STORY

Back in 1992, Mattel, the toy company, generated more publicity than it intended when it introduced Teen Talk Barbie, a talking doll. Among the things that the doll said was, "Math is hard." The line prompted such a public outcry from educational groups that Mattel deleted it from the voice boxes of the Barbies on the assembly line.

Barbie's math anxiety wouldn't have caused such a stir if it hadn't tapped into a collective cultural anxiety about girls and math. Authorities far more scholarly than Barbie have echoed her controversial statement that girls find math class tough. And some scientists have gone as far as to suggest that girls are biologically inferior at math, perhaps because of some "math gene" on the Y chromosome.

No math gene has ever been found. Still, for some reason, boys do better on standardized math tests, and their advantage increases over time. Take, for example, the National Assessment of Educational Progress, an exam given on a voluntary basis to fourth, eighth, and twelfth graders around the country. In the test given to fourth graders in 1996, about 5 percent of the boys and 3 percent of the girls scored 5 out of a possible 6. None got a 6. Of the twelfth graders, slightly more boys than girls scored 5, but 10 percent of the boys got the top score, compared with 5 percent of the girls.

Although the gender gap in math has closed somewhat in

recent decades, the basic pattern hasn't changed. In 1995, an analysis of thirty-two years of test scores found that boys outnumbered girls 3 to 1 among the top 10 percent scorers. This pattern shows up in other countries, too. The Third International Mathematics and Science Study, an achievement test, was given in 1995 and 1996 to half a million students in forty-one countries who were in the equivalent of the fourth, eighth, and twelfth grades. The boys did better than the girls in the math and science portions of the test in all countries except South Africa, and the gap increased with age.

Before going any further, let's put the gender differences in math test scores in perspective. There is much more variation *among* girls and *among* boys than there is *between* girls and boys. And girls' lag behind boys is minuscule compared to the much-publicized lag of students in the United States behind students in many other industrialized countries. A comparison of fifth graders in the United States, Japan, and Taiwan on one math test found that the American boys scored only a quarter of a point higher, on average, than the American girls, but that the Asian students scored 9 to 10 points higher than the American students.

However small it is, the persistent gender difference in standardized test scores seems to make a pretty convincing case that boys are fundamentally better than girls in math. But breaking down the scores only by gender doesn't tell the whole story. Recently, researchers have started breaking down the scores by some ethnic groups, and they've found that the gender gap applies to white students but not to blacks and Hispanics. The fact that the gender difference isn't found across the board calls into question the idea that boys *as a group* are better at math.

There are two other monkey wrenches in the long-standing stereotype about boys, girls, and math. For one thing, even though white boys get better total scores than white girls on standardized math tests, boys aren't better at all kinds of math questions. Girls have a slight edge in doing basic calculations, like addition and subtraction. And girls of all backgrounds get better grades in math in school. You could chalk this finding up to social factors, such as girls being more diligent about studying or to an occasional teacher's preference for girls, except that girls maintain this advantage from elementary school through graduate school. "You can't have it both ways," said Carol Beal. "If boys' brains are really better for math, they should be doing better in math."

Bias in Standardized Tests

Unfortunately for girls, the standardized math tests that they do worst on are the ones that count the most: the PSATs and the SATs. The PSATs, taken by high school sophomores and juniors around the country, determine who will be semifinalists for the 7,400 prestigious and lucrative National Merit Scholarships for college. The SATs, taken by high school juniors, influence which colleges will accept them. The PSATs and SATs have two parts: math and verbal. Boys get higher overall scores on these tests, but the math score accounts for most of the difference. In 1996, boys' average combined SAT scores were 1,040 and girls' were 998 out of a possible 1,600. The average math SAT score for boys was 531, and for girls it was just 496 out of a possible 800.

The SATs are supposed to predict a student's performance in college, but girls do better in college than their SAT scores predict and boys do worse. So the SATs and PSATs are widely seen as biased against girls. The Educational Testing Service, which produces the PSATs and SATs, has been trying to eliminate bias in its tests for nearly two decades. The company asks educators to review the scores to see if any of the questions were answered correctly by the majority of boys and wrong by the majority of girls, or vice versa. The educators also look for imbalances according to race. Questions with answers that are skewed strongly in favor of one sex or a particular race are not used again.

In reviewing the answers, the testing service has found that the details used in math word problems have a lot to do with whether boys or girls will get them right. For example, boys do better on math problems that are couched in sports terms—the number of yards that a quarterback has to run, for example—than on problems framed in terms of, say, the yards of material needed to make a dress. For girls, the reverse is true. So gender differences in interests and hobbies affect gender differences in math scores.

The Educational Testing Service realized that one way to reduce gender bias on the college entrance tests was to avoid questions that refer to strongly male or female interests. But rather than guess what these interests are, the company decided to find out scientifically. It distributed questionnaires to students asking what they like to do outside school. To no one's surprise, the questionnaires showed considerable overlap between boys and girls, but also some notable differences. Boys said that they spent more time playing sports, for instance, and girls said that they devoted more time to "social" or "aesthetic" pursuits, like trying on clothes or just talking with friends.

Since the Educational Testing Service began rooting out biased questions, the gender gap in the tests' scores has narrowed. But to narrow the gap even more, the company recently tried another approach: It added an essay question to the PSATs. Traditionally, the PSATs and SATs were made up exclusively of multiple-choice questions. But girls do better than boys on writing tests. With the addition of the essay question in 1997, the gap favoring boys dropped to 2.7 points from 4.5 points in the previous year.

Math Is Hard: A Self-fulfilling Prophecy

Gender bias in standardized tests is just one of the difficulties girls have with math. Another is an attitude problem. By early adolescence, many girls start thinking of themselves as being poor at math. Whatever interest they had in math takes a dive, so many of them want to stop taking math as soon as they fulfill the minimum requirement. Many boys also lose interest in math at this time, but the change is more dramatic for girls.

Dropping math classes wouldn't be so bad were it not for the fact that math, more than subjects like, say, social studies or French, is a meal ticket. High school students who aren't well grounded in math can't major in subjects like economics or the sciences in college (unless they take catch-up math courses in college), which means that they're locked out of professional training in areas like business and medicine that lead to high-paying careers. Put simply, high school students who don't take more than the minimum requirement of math end up making less money than do students who go beyond the minimum.

If girls do as well as boys in math classes, why do they lose confidence in their ability to handle math? Why do they come to dislike math? Many girls, no doubt, are reacting to a well-documented attitude of their peers—that being good in math makes girls seem unattractive to boys. Another factor is that even in the post–Title IX decades, girls get less attention and support from their teachers. Studies have found that teachers call on boys more often and respond more often to boys' requests for help when they teach math.

Patricia Campbell, an educational consultant with a special interest in girls and math, said that some teachers give the girls in their class less critical feedback on their math work because of a mistaken belief that if they challenge the girls too much, they'll discourage them. But, she said, without tough feedback, girls don't get the experience of failing and then bouncing back and learning from their mistakes. So, when they struggle with a problem or do poorly on a test, girls are more apt than boys to jump to the conclusion that they're bad at math.

Then there's the matter of subtle gender bias at home. Jacquelynne Eccles and Janis Jacobs, of the University of Michigan at Ann Arbor, have followed thousands of children since the early 1980s in an attempt to understand the roots of gender differences in interest and performance in math and other subjects. They've given questionnaires to students in elementary school through high school asking what they thought of math. They've given questionnaires to parents asking whether they thought there were sex differences in math ability and how they rated their children's math ability. They've assessed the children's math ability by talking to the children's teachers and looking at their grades and standardized test scores.

Most of the parents started out believing that their sons and daughters were equally competent in math. And, on average, their views didn't change as their children moved from elementary school to middle school and high school. But beginning when their children were in the sixth grade, some parents— those who tended to think that, as Barbie suggested, math class is tough for girls—underestimated their daughters' math ability and overestimated their sons'. Parents whose daughters were in the top of their class in math had a ready explanation: Their daughters worked hard. Parents whose sons excelled in math attributed their performance to natural talent.

Did the girls really have to work harder than the boys to get the same scores? The teachers didn't think so. But just to be sure, the researchers used an objective measure: the amount of time the children spent on math schoolwork and homework. Eccles and Jacobs saw no difference.

Even though the girls didn't need to put extra effort into math, Eccles and Jacobs noticed that the parents who doubted their daughters' math ability had subtle ways of letting their view slip out. When a girl had a question about her math homework, the mother or father might say, "That's a tough one," instead of something more positive like, "You can do it." Or when the girl did well on a math test, a parent might say, "You studied really hard," instead of something like, "I'm not surprised. You're good in math." Regardless of how the message was delivered, the researchers found that it created a self-fulfilling prophecy. The daughters came to doubt how good they really were at math, even if they were getting top grades.

Of course, it's unfair to lay all the blame on parents when their daughters think they're weak in math. Sometimes a girl's self-doubt comes from within. Rachel was a strong math student. She got good grades and scored above the 90th percentile in a standardized math test given to third graders in New York City. Even so, when she was in the fifth grade, she told her parents that she didn't think she was good at math.

Rachel's parents were surprised. They thought that they'd done everything they could to support Rachel's interest and talent in math. Her mother was especially sensitive to the stereotype about girls and math because she thought that it was damaging to her as a student. She recalled wanting to drop math as soon as she could in high school and that her parents, her guidance counselor, and her teachers did nothing to change her mind. Looking back, she wished that she had taken more math classes.

When Rachel's mother asked her why she didn't think she was good in math, Rachel said that it was because she had to work hard at it. She compared herself to a boy in her class who seemed to be able to do math effortlessly. Did she notice the boy's gift for math because she expected to see it—because he was a boy? Rachel's mother remembered having been intimidated by boys in her class who got the answer faster, so she didn't know how to bolster her daughter's confidence.

When told about Rachel, Eccles had an idea. "The parents need to be careful not to let their daughter keep our culture's belief that if you've got to work harder you're not as good," Eccles said. "The parents should tell her that maybe the particular kind of math that their daughter and this boy were doing comes more easily to him, but that doesn't mean that all math comes more easily to him. The parents should also say that math is a subject where at some points you have to work harder and then it becomes easier."

While it's certainly true that starting algebra or trigonometry or any kind of math can be a struggle for anybody, there's some research to suggest that one particular kind of math problem really is more of a struggle for girls. The research isn't conclusive, and it doesn't mean that boys are better at math overall. But it shows that girls have to work harder than boys to solve algebra word problems. These problems ask students to compare two quantities: Allen has 10 apples. He has 8 apples less than Lily. How many apples does Lily have?

In studying how boys and girls work out this sort of problem, David Geary said that boys see a picture of the problem in their heads. It may go something like this: 10 apples under Allen's name and then 10 + 8 under Lily's name. So they can visualize that the answer is 18. Girls, on the other hand, try to puzzle out the answer by studying the words, and many girls get tripped up on the "less than" part. So more girls than boys make the mistake of subtracting 8 from 10 to get 2, the wrong answer. Geary thinks that boys' ability to turn the word problem into a picture may be related to their strength in some spatial skills.

But Geary has found that one simple trick can put girls on an equal footing with boys in figuring out the problems. For girls who need the extra help, parents and teachers should show them how to diagram word problems on paper. For the problem just mentioned, the diagram would be $X - 8 = 10$. He said that studies show that diagramming on paper doesn't affect boys' scores on these problems, but it does improve girls' scores. Geary tested the strategy at home when his daughter was having difficulty with algebra, and it worked for her.

Closing the Math Gap

It remains to be seen how Rachel will progress with math. But if other girls' experiences are any indication, there's a good chance that she'll stick with it through high school. In the past few years, the gender gap in math has been closing. Girls now take as many high school credits of math as boys—about 3.5. As many girls as boys take algebra, geometry, trigonometry, and precalculus classes. So, it would seem that girls' long-standing handicap in math was more sociological than biological.

One reason why girls are taking more math is that all students are taking more math. States and school districts around the country have instituted tougher standards in many core subjects to meet the federal government's mandate to improve education. For example, in 1990, 12 states required high school students to take at least 2.5 credits in math to graduate. By 1996, 18 states had this requirement. But more rigorous standards don't completely explain the strides that girls have made in math. There's also less gender bias in the classroom. Textbooks include more female characters than they used to. And teachers are more conscious of calling on girls as often as boys.

In addition, math curricula have changed in ways that girls may find more engaging. There are numerous curricula geared to teaching math to girls. Though there's been no independent evaluation of them, one element that educators agree is effective is the emphasis on doing something that should have been done years ago—making math interesting. The National Council of Teachers in Math, which develops standards for teaching math, recognizes that for too long, math was taught as a collection of disconnected facts. To make math more engaging to more students, the council emphasizes the need to make it relevant to their experiences. While the brightest, most highly motivated math students may have done fine with the old style of math work sheets, Eccles said that the newer, hands-on curricula pull in the other students, girls as well as boys.

In my son's elementary school, the mantra is "everyday math." Children don't just learn how to add and subtract; they learn these concepts in the context of using money in a store or bidding on items in a classroom auction. Students make up "number stories" (Tom had 12 chocolate kisses. Three friends came over. How many chocolate kisses did each child get?) as a means of understanding the many ways that numbers relate to daily life.

Hundreds of public and private elementary and secondary schools around the country have adopted the EQUALS, a highly regarded math curriculum that uses many techniques to reach out to girls and other students who may feel that they're not good at math. With the curriculum, teachers create a supportive environment in which all students are encouraged to take risks by tackling and persisting with tough math problems. Instead of filling out work sheets, students break up into groups and solve math problems using all the tools of mathematics: calculators, blocks, computers, diagrams, and graphs. To maintain students' interest and motivation, EQUALS involves the families with seminars that show them how to incorporate math problem solving into everyday activities.

Although girls' progress in math is hailed as one of the great success stories in achieving gender equity in school, more work remains. Boys still outnumber girls in calculus, the most demanding high school math course. As Campbell sees it, perhaps the biggest gender gap in math today is not one of opportunity but one of interest. No matter how many math courses they take and how well they do, girls still don't like math as much as boys do. Campbell thinks that the reason has less to do with what goes on in school than what goes on outside school. Girls have fewer interests that allow them to see the everyday applications of math, a prime example being computers.

THE TECHNOLOGY GAP

A generation ago, computers were marginalized into one room in the high school, and groups of boys could be seen hunched around a behemoth machine as it spit out a reams of arcane data. Obviously, a lot has changed. Computer classes are mandatory in many schools starting in kindergarten. At home, personal computers and Internet connections are fast becoming as common as TV sets. Computer literacy seems less a gender issue than a generation issue, with many parents joking that when they've got a computer question, they ask their children.

But despite the veneer of equality, boys still have far more interest in and experience with computers. Most computer games are bought for boys because most of the games are made for boys— they've got mainly male characters and their competitive, shoot-em-up action appeals more to boys. Even educational software has more male than female characters. The overabundance of software for boys wouldn't be a problem were it not for the fact that playing computer games is how children first learn about—and learn to like—computers.

It's not surprising, then, that surveys show that boys find computers more enjoyable and interesting than girls do and are more inclined to visit the computer exhibits in science museums. Many girls manage to overcome initial feelings of inadequacy on the computer in elementary school, when all students are required to learn basics like getting onto the Internet and using educational software. But research shows a significant difference in high school, when technology courses are optional.

At the very time when many girls are losing interest and confidence in their ability to handle high-level math and science courses, the same thing is happening with computer classes. By high school, the computer classes that girls take tend to be relatively low-level data-entry courses. It's mainly boys who are enrolling in advanced computer science and graphics courses, the kind that prepare them for high-level jobs in information technology and even lucrative part-time jobs as they work their ways though college. "The failure to include girls in advanced-level computer science courses threatens to make women bystanders in the technological 21st century," stated a 1998 report by the American Association of University Women Educational Foundation, a research group.

The AAUW report blamed gender bias in educational software. It cited research on elementary school math software that found that only 12 percent of the gender-identifiable characters were female and that most of the females were portrayed as passive mothers or princesses. "Not surprisingly, given the emphasis on technology as a masculine domain, many girls in high school forgo the opportunity to take computing classes that could lead to technology careers," the AAUW report stated.

"With girls, you've got to really work at getting them interested in computers," said Kaveri Subrahmanyam, a psychologist at California State University who studies gender differences in computer use. But as a parent, Subrahmanyam knows firsthand just how hard this can be. "I haven't done a very good job with my daughter," she admits. Her 10-year-old daughter doesn't like computer games, even those marketed for girls. "The only time she became interested in computers is when her friend got E-mail," Subrahmanyam said. "So, we got her an E-mail account."

Like many girls, Subrahamanyam's daughter is more interested in the Internet than in computer games. While not long ago boys used the Internet in far greater numbers than girls, girls have nearly caught up. Subrahmanyam thinks that the reason why girls are flocking to the Internet is that it offers them more of what they want from computers—a means of accomplishing something, be it chatting, sending E-mail, or doing research. "Boys are interested in computers themselves," she said. "For some boys, this interest borders on an obsession. But girls like using computers as a tool rather than as an end in and of itself." So, boys are techies and girls want to know, What can the computer do for me?

Consider the different ways that boys and girls use the Internet. Subrahmanyam said that boys do more surfing, girls more chatting, communicating. Janna, a 12 year old in Connecticut, has been using the Internet for several years. By the time she was 10, she would come home from school, turn on the computer, and chat with children from around the world. At age 11, she created her own web page.

It's hard to imagine computer-savvy girls like Janna entering high school with the technology anxiety of their older sisters. Just as higher education and aspirations elevated an earlier generation of women above the typing pool, richer and more complex experiences with computers in elementary school are bound to help girls do more with computers than type their papers. But it'll take more than mandatory computer classes to make more girls *like* computers.

Some schools are taking steps to help make computers more appealing to girls. They go out of their way to hire women to teach computer classes in the hope that a female role model will make a difference. At the Manhattan Country School, a private school in New York City, teachers also keep their eyes open for boys dominating girls when they work in pairs on computer projects. When they notice a boy doing the hands-on computer work and a girl sitting passively or simply writing down what the boy does, the teachers intervene and make sure that each student gets equal time on the computer. To close the gender gap in technology, parents and teachers may be able to learn from the progress made so far in closing the gender gap in sports.

THE SPORTS GAP

More girls are involved in sports today than at any other time in U.S. history. More than one out of every 3 high school girls participates in sports, up from only 1 in 27 in 1971. Along with traditionally female sports like swimming and field hockey, the sports with the most girls playing now are basketball, track and field, volleyball, softball, and soccer. Female sporting events pack stadiums and gymnasiums with crowds that were unimaginable just a few years ago.

But there's more work to be done in closing the gender gap in sports. If you look behind the newspaper articles lauding the stellar female athletes, you'll see that girls still face hurdles in sports at all levels. Many girls who enthusiastically join co-ed sports teams find the same sort of gender bias that kept their mothers off the field. Boys don't pass balls to them or they criticize the way the girls play. Coaches often don't take the boys to task for these insults, preferring to let the children work out their own conflicts. Margaret was gung-ho about Little League when she was 6, but she dropped out when she was 8 because the number of girls had dwindled, the boys were dominating the field, and she was spending a lot of time on the bench. She'd like to play on a girls-only team, but her town has them only for older girls.

Surveys show that most parents think that sports are equally important for boys and girls. But when push comes to shove, many would just as soon avoid the kind of aggravation Margaret encountered. Rather than fight gender bias in Little League, many parents find it easier to enroll their daughters in traditionally female activities like gymnastics or dance classes, as Margaret's parents did. One mother got a kick out of her daughter playing tee ball, but she admitted to being relieved when Lisa didn't want to sign up the following year. "A lot of the girls were dropping out," the mother said. "Besides, it was a pain giving up my Saturdays for all those games."

If some parents are quietly relieved when their daughters quit a team, it may be because they didn't have much confidence in their athletic ability in the first place. Eccles and Jacobs found that many parents think their daughters aren't good at sports. They rate their daughters' ability as being lower than it really is on the basis of their performance. And they rate their sons' ability as being better than it really is. As is the case with math, many girls pick up on their parents' attitudes and then lose confidence in themselves and lose interest in sports.

Of course, it's not all the parents' fault. Many parents are committed to doing whatever they can to help their daughters stick with sports. And girls still have to battle out-and-out discrimination. Consider what happened recently to a girls' soccer team in suburban Indianapolis. The team was practicing before a game when a boys' soccer team showed up. It turns out that there had been a scheduling conflict and both the boys' and the girls' teams were slated to practice on the same field at the same time. The boys' coach told the girls to move to another, less desirable field. Some of the girls said that it was unfair for them to have to move since they were there first. But the boys' coach insisted, and the girls' coach told his team to pack up.

"I've seen this sort of thing happen with two boys' teams, and it always ends up that the team that got to the field last had to find another field to play on," said Melissa, the mother of a player on the girls' team, who tried unsuccessfully to convince both coaches that the girls had the right to stay. Evidently, the coaches thought that the girls' team was less important than the boys' team.

Afterward, Melissa talked privately to her daughter's coach. She told him that his action made the girls feel that they were inferior to the boys. The coach said that he hadn't thought of the situation that way—that he was simply trying to avoid a conflict. But said that he wouldn't let it happen again.

With any luck, Melissa's daughter's coach will go on to help reduce bias against girls in sports. It's a gradual process, which often involves winning converts one at a time. In its report on gender gaps at school, the AAUW described how the girls' basketball team at a rural southern high school helped turn around the faculty's traditional assumptions about gender roles. Watching the team play one day, a teacher gestured to one of the players and said to the coach, "She's a cocky little thing." It was unclear whether the teacher's statement was intended as a compliment (as in, "She's a good player.") or as an insult (as in, "She's unfeminine.").

The coach's response was emphatically praiseworthy. "You have to have a certain confidence to play," the coach said.

The conversation expanded to a discussion of the faculty's mixed reactions to the athletic girls. Although these girls were clearly leaders among their peers and full of self-confidence, some faculty members were initially uncomfortable seeing girls with such traditionally "unfeminine" qualities. But as they got used to seeing the girls play and listening to coaches praise them, the teachers gradually stopped judging the players' femininity and focused on their skill—and the pride their skill brought to the school.

That day, one more teacher was won over.

THE SPECIAL EDUCATION GAP

As with sports, there have long been gender differences in special education, classes that provide extra help to students in reading and other subjects. For generations, it has been an unquestioned fact that more boys than girls need special ed— two-thirds of the children in special ed are boys. But several years ago, Sally and Bennett Shaywitz, experts on reading disabilities at Yale, began asking whether learning disabilities really were more common in boys. The overabundance of boys in special ed seemed odd, given that there were as many boys as girls at the top of the class. Could boys' performance at school really be so much more variable than girls'?

The Shaywitzes focused on dyslexia, the most common reading disability and the main reason for referrals to special ed. They followed 414 students in Connecticut when they were in second and third grades. For the study, the students were evaluated for dyslexia twice: once by the schools and again by trained researchers. The Shaywitzes wanted to see how reliable the schools' diagnoses were compared with the researchers' more accurate diagnoses. In both grade levels, the schools identified dyslexia in too many boys and too few girls. For example, the schools pronounced that about 14 percent of the second-grade boys and 3 percent of the second-grade girls had the reading disability, when, in fact, 9 percent of the boys and 7 percent of the girls actually had it.

The Shaywitzes took a closer look at the children and noticed a striking difference between the boys who were identified by the teachers and the boys whom the teachers considered normal. More of the identified boys had behavioral problems. The Shaywitzes then realized that the researchers were mistaking behavioral problems for reading problems.

Boys do misbehave more than girls. They're wilder, they get into more physical fights, and they're less likely to do as the teacher says. One reason is that they're more prone to attention deficit-hyperactivity disorder, a developmental disorder that causes wild, impulsive, and often combative behavior and difficulty concentrating. Girls get ADHD, too, but for them the main symptom is difficulty concentrating, not disruptive behavior. No one knows why ADHD affects boys and girls in different ways. (For a more detailed discussion on gender differences in ADHD, see Chapter 5, pages 211–14.)

Even many boys who don't have ADHD tend to have more trouble than girls sitting still and concentrating, especially in the early years of elementary school. They shout out answers instead of raising their hands. When they're supposed to sit up straight in a circle on the floor, they sprawl out as if they're in their own living rooms. Experts think that this restlessness is due to boys' lag in self-control, which some researchers estimate is about six months behind girls' at the start of kindergarten. But boys' misbehavior also relates to the nature of boys' social inter- actions. In watching boys and girls in class, several researchers have observed that boys are more interested in pleasing one another than in pleasing the teacher. And pleasing one another often means doing something "bad," like sword fighting with pencils or making funny noises.

Whatever the reason for boys' unruly behavior, the Shaywitzes found that it contributed to a referral bias for special ed at school. Boys were overdiagnosed with dyslexia and girls were underdiagnosed. Misbehavior may not have been the only factor. Many researchers think that boys do learn to read more slowly than girls. But being slow to read isn't the same thing as having a reading disability.

The gender bias in diagnosing children with reading disabil- ities is bad for the boys and the girls. It means that many boys get remedial reading instruction that they don't need— and that teachers expect less of them than they can give. And it means that many girls who need extra help aren't getting it, so their reading difficulties get worse. Indeed, the Shaywitzes found that most of the girls with reading disabilities weren't identified until the disabilities were especially severe.

The older a child is when diagnosed with dyslexia, the smaller the chance that the child will ever read normally, said G. Reid Lyons, of the National Institute of Child and Human Development. Although the problem of late diagnosis is most common in girls, it affects boys, too. Lyons said that in most cases reading disabilities aren't identified until a child is in the third grade, but by then there's just a 25 percent chance that the child's reading skills can be brought up to average. If that child is helped in the first grade, he or she has a 95 percent chance of becoming a normal reader by the end of the second grade.

There's a way to close the gender gap in the diagnosis of reading disabilities and help make sure that all children with reading disabilities are identified early enough. Lyons would like to see all children given an informal screening test for reading difficulty at the end of kindergarten or at the beginning of the first grade. The test is easy enough to be done by the child's teacher in class or even by a parent at home. All it takes is watching the child read some words and seeing how well he or she breaks the words into sounds—what experts call phonological processing, the nuts and bolts of reading. Most 5 and 6 year olds get confused about some of the letter sounds, especially the vowels. But extreme difficulty with most of the letter sounds is a red flag of a reading disability, Lyons said. The solution is to give these children one-on-one instruction in phonics, or sounding out words, for about half an hour a day.

BIAS AGAINST BOYS

The headmistress of a formerly all-girls school in the Northeast that recently went co-ed was eating lunch in the school cafeteria when she noticed an empty table littered with paper cups, napkins, and lunch trays. A school rule is that students must clean up their tables. The headmistress asked the girls at the next table who had been sitting at the messy one. "Some boys," they said.

The headmistress frowned. She said that the trouble that the boys caused at school was out of proportion to their number. Most of the students who got detention and other punishments were boys, yet just 40 percent of the students were boys. The headmistress said that the school had no plans to make the boy-girl ratio any higher because, as she put it, "You know what they say—it takes the 60 percent of the class who are female to keep the rest in line."

Most teachers and principals aren't as candid as the head-mistress. They don't come out and say that boys are more diffi-cult than girls. They put a positive spin on the boys, describing them as spirited or energetic. But the way they treat the boys in their classrooms may more accurately reflect the headmistress' words than their own. Judith Klienfeld, a psychologist at the University of Alaska in Fairbanks, is one of several researchers who think that schools are biased against boys. Evidently, most children think so, too. In a national survey of three thousand fourth to tenth graders sponsored by the AAUW, most of the boys as well as the girls said that teachers preferred girls.

Whether most teachers really do prefer girls, it's easy to see how children could get that impression. Schools reward the kinds of behavior that come more easily to girls than to boys. From the first day of kindergarten, teachers expect students to sit still and pay attention, to raise their hands when they want to speak, and to form a straight line when they walk through the school. Who can blame them? But, as we've already seen, boys as a group misbehave more than girls. So teachers spend more time reprimanding boys: "Raise your hand," "Sit up straight," "Be quiet." Or, in extreme cases, "Go to the principal's office!"

Of course, many boys shape up and deliver what the teacher wants for fear of being punished. But those who don't are at risk of low achievement. They play the "bad boy" role that the teachers expect of them. Teachers often interpret a boy's misbe-havior as a sign of ADHD and recommend that he have a psy-chological evaluation. ADHD is more common in boys than in girls, but doctors have found that it's not nearly as common in boys as teachers think, based on the volume of their referrals. The teachers may also peg many of the misbehaving boys as slow learners and put them in remedial classes. Either way, the boys feel stigmatized. They lose faith in themselves as students and often stop trying anywhere near their best.

Some psychologists think that the biases against boys at school help explain the grim realities of their school records. More boys than girls have to repeat a grade. And more boys end up dropping out of high school.

No doubt, many factors contribute to boys' high rate of school failure. But some experts think that boys would do better in school and misbehave less if schools were more sensitive to their needs—especially their need to get up and move around. Instead of punishing students for not sitting still, why not restructure lessons so that they don't have to sit still for long stretches?

Faye Chaplain, who teaches a prekindergarten class made up largely of boys at the Community Nursery School in Dobbs Ferry, New York, said that when her former students come back to visit, many have the same complaint about kindergarten: They have very little time to get outside and run around. In nursery school, they played outside for an hour each day; in kindergarten, they get about twenty minutes. And the meager twenty minutes of recess is cut down to nothing in the increasing number of schools around the country that are abandoning recess in an attempt to increase academic standards and lower their insurance liability. Chaplain worries about boys who aren't given enough opportunity to burn off excess energy because she knows from experience that boys who are cooped up for too long often use their pent-up energy to act out.

William Pollack, a psychologist at Harvard Medical School, points to research demonstrating what Chaplain has observed—that many boys who are "straitjacketed" by being forced to sit indoors for too long tend to be wild and disobedient or to withdraw mentally from the classroom. Many of them are normal boys who misbehave out of boredom or frustration, he said, but they are labeled as "conduct disordered" or "troublemakers" or diagnosed with "hyperactivity." In his book, *Real Boys*, Pollack also described boys who were seen as problems in one school but who went on to flourish in schools that understood boys' needs and built more activity into the school day. Many of these schools were either all-boys' schools or had single-sex classes for certain subjects that aimed to cater to boys' and girls' different paces and styles of learning.

IS SINGLE-SEX EDUCATION THE ANSWER?

It's clear that boys and girls have different needs in school and that they face different crisis points along the way. And with recent research showing that boys are often shortchanged at the expense of girls and that girls are often shortchanged at the expense of boys, many educators and parents wonder if children are better off in single-sex schools or classes. Some children who attend co-ed schools wonder the same thing.

"I wish I could be in a math class without boys," said Kara, a tenth grader in a New York suburb. Because Kara understands the importance of math, she is determined to take math through the end of high school. But, she said: "I don't really like taking math because of the boys. The boys are so much quicker in math. They call out the answers. I sit in the back and don't say anything."

So, increasing numbers of co-ed public and private schools are offering single-sex classes. The biggest push has been for girls' classes in math and science. Advocates of these classes point to research showing that boys tend to do precisely what

Kara said: They dominate the class by shouting out answers, leaving girls either too intimidated to raise their hands or feeling, why bother? The hope is that in girls-only classes, girls will get more attention, feel more confident, and do better in these subjects. Advocates for boys-only classes think that some boys will learn better if they're not compared unfavorably to the more mature, better-behaved girls and if teachers understand boys greater need for physical activity.

But are children's needs really met better by single-sex classes? To find out, the AAUW marshaled a group of leading educational scholars to look at studies of students in kindergarten through the twelfth grade who attended co-ed schools and single-sex schools, as well as students in co-ed schools that held some single-sex classes. The studies compared how the students fared in these settings: how happy they were in school and how well they did. Most of the studies were about girls, but some information emerged about boys, too.

The findings were mixed. There were some benefits from single-sex schools and classes, but overall they were no better than co-ed classes and schools. Single-sex schools as a group were no less likely than co-ed schools as a group to reinforce many of the traditional gender stereotypes. The report stated that boys seemed less affected one way or the other by the sex-composition of the students than by the sex composition of the teachers. It found that boys suffered a lower "overall sense of well-being" in schools where most of the teachers were female compared with those in schools with more male teachers. Male teachers are scarce in elementary schools, but they're probably scarcer in co-ed schools than in all-boys' schools.

The report found some clear benefits from girls' schools and classes. Girls who attended them were more satisfied with their schools than were girls in co-ed schools without any girls' classes. In particular, girls in single-sex environments were less likely to see math and science as "masculine" and enjoyed these courses more than did girls in co-ed schools. But there was a paradox. The girls in single-sex classes in co-ed schools didn't do better in math and science. So, the experts concluded that single-sex classes are not magic bullets of gender equity.

The performance of girls in girls' schools—as opposed to girls' classes in co-ed schools—was more questionable. In many cases, these girls did better on standardized tests. But the difference appeared to have less to do with the absence of boys than with other qualities that are common to girls' schools. Compared with co-ed schools, the girls' schools studied were smaller, had more rigorous curricula, and had students from families with higher incomes and educational levels. These are ingredients for academic success at *any* school. So, it would stand to reason that girls in girls' schools would have higher test scores than would girls in other schools. The question is, How can some of the elements of the best girls' schools be incorporated into co-ed schools to benefit both girls and boys?

TOWARD GENDER EQUITY AT SCHOOL

Many public and co-ed private schools around the country have adopted "gender-equity" programs in an effort to reduce gender biases in the classroom. When such programs first emerged several years ago, they were synonymous with helping girls, but now the focus is on improving education for all students. At most schools, gender-equity efforts involve little more than a discussion during a staff development session on the importance of making sure to give equal attention to boys and girls in the classroom. But some schools have gone considerably further, drawing on the advice of gender-equity committees of their Parent-Teacher Associations, sending teachers to gender-equity conferences, and even hiring consultants to critique their classrooms and curricula.

At Ethical Culture, a co-ed private school in Manhattan, an educational consultant videotaped elementary school classes so that teachers could see whether they were really treating the boys and girls fairly. The teachers, aware that research had long shown that teachers tend to pay more attention to boys, assumed that they'd solved that problem. But when they played back the tapes, the teachers were surprised to learn that they hadn't. The videos showed that the teachers were giving the most attention to the most talkative boys. Realizing that they couldn't trust their instincts alone, the teachers devised systems, like calling on two boys and then two girls, to make sure that they gave the girls and boys equal attention.

Nearly one thousand public and private schools around the country have sent teachers to seminars given by SEED, an organization started by researchers at Wellesley College in Massachusetts whose full name hints at its mission: Seeking Educational Equity and Diversity. The seminars don't dictate curricular changes or espouse teaching techniques. Rather, their goal is to help teachers become more sensitive to gender and racial biases and to figure out how best to eliminate them in their own classrooms.

It's hard to imagine any school trying harder to achieve gender equity than the Manhattan Country School, a progressive private school on New York City's Upper East Side for children in preschool through the eighth grade. Manhattan Country had always striven for racial equity, but like most other schools, it hadn't thought much about gender equity until nearly a decade ago. Gus Trowbridge, a former director of the school, recalled the turning point. The father of a sixth grader remarked to

Trowbridge at a year-end conference, "If a student at the Manhattan Country School called another student a nigger, the offender would be in your office in a flash, but I'll bet nothing would happen to someone calling a classmate a faggot."

At first, Trowbridge took offense to the statement, but he soon realized that the parent was right. "Sexist slurs were commonplace in our classrooms and corridors," he wrote in a school newsletter. But such remarks "were largely ignored, or if noted with objection by teachers, students passed them off as teasing, claiming they did no harm. When challenged that they wouldn't use racial slurs so freely, children insisted that the two were not the same. The fact is we hadn't taught them that they *were* the same."

So, in 1991 the Manhattan Country School received a grant to begin a gender-equity program that would permeate the academic and social life of the school. The school made curricular changes in an effort to close the gender gaps in math and reading. To improve boys' adjustment to school, the school hired several male teachers. And to sustain boys' interest in reading and writing, teachers made sure to offer them books with strong male characters. Noticing that girls were losing interest in physical education as they got into the upper grades, the school broadened the physical education curriculum to include units in karate and African dance, along with the more traditional units in competitive sports.

Many of these curricular changes are commonplace at public and private schools around the country, but what sets Manhattan Country School's gender-equity project apart is its reach into what one teacher calls the "hallway curriculum." In other words, teachers are alert to offhanded sexist remarks and activities in the hallways and on the playground, and they bring instances of gender bias up for class discussions. Martha Foote, a former head teacher of the 4- and 5 year olds, was disturbed by the budding sexism she saw in the classic game of chase—groups of preschool boys chasing preschool girls on the playground. She spoke to the children at circle time, explaining that she thought it was unfair to split up into groups or teams based on physical traits. "I announced that I would feel terrible if I wanted to be a 'chaser' in the chase game, but was told that I couldn't because I was a girl," Foote wrote in the school newsletter.

"Hands flew into the air as each child wished to relate an injustice directed at her or him and the hurt feelings which ensued," she continued. The children then decided that they would no longer play chase as the girls against the boys but rather would ask classmates beforehand whether they wanted to be a chaser or one of the chased. That plan worked for a while, but eventually the children lapsed into the traditional pattern of the boys chasing the girls. At that point, Foote changed the rules of the game. Teams were divided equally among boys and girls, and the teams switched back and forth from being the chasers to being the chased.

"The revamped chase was a hit," Foote wrote. "Children who had forever seemed destined to be chasees were now experiencing the thrill of being the chasers. Likewise, the former chasers were discovering the satisfaction of thwarting their pursuers. For the first time, it seemed that everyone felt the game was truly theirs to play. And they were having a ball."

Did this playground lesson ensure perfect gender harmony in the years ahead? Not quite. Sexist remarks and activities still occur, but teachers and parents say that they have diminished. By the third year of the gender-equity project, Valerie Gutwirth, a former teacher of 7- and 8 year olds, said, "I rarely heard the word *fag* or *gay* used as an insult; when I did, often another child would not let it pass unremarked."

In addition to trying to eliminate sexism, teachers help students to recognize and break free of gender-stereotyped behavior in themselves. Carol O'Donnell, who teaches the seventh and eighth grades, said that she sometimes needs to encourages girls to "get over their resistance to getting involved in a conflict or an intellectual debate" and boys to "share their feelings." She admits that the latter is more of a challenge, but she said that one assignment was especially successful.

The class had read *The Color of Water*, a black man's biography of his white mother and a tribute to her. After the class had finished the book, O'Donnell gave the students a homework assignment to write a love letter to someone. Although it wasn't required, several of the children wanted to read their love letters to the class the next day. One of these students was a boy who had previously shown what O'Donnell considered to be a disturbing lack of empathy—he had made a joke to some classmates about someone who was killed in an accident. But this same boy stood up in front of the class and read his love letter to his mother. This took courage, O'Donnell said, but the boy knew that he would be respected, not ridiculed, for exposing his feelings.

Will this boy be as willing to bear his soul at the high school he attends upon graduation from Manhattan Country School? Whichever school that is, it's certain to be more like the real world of sexist teasing and gender stereotyping. Whether this boy will become more like his new classmates remains to be seen, but the experiences of other graduates offer some hope.

At an alumni gathering, some former students talked frankly about their culture shock in the gender-biased environments of their high schools. But several also told how they held onto the values they learned at Manhattan Country. One boy said that he refused to make friends with classmates who were sexist. After the gathering, Michael Neal, the father of a boy at Manhattan Country School, said that his son took a more activist approach.

No sooner did he start attending an elite private high school in Manhattan, where, as Neal put it, "the emphasis on gender equity didn't exist," then the boy began plotting what he could do to change the school.

SUMMING UP

Tremendous strides have been made in reducing gender bias in education. Perhaps the greatest success story is that the long-standing math gap, in which girls scored lower than boys on standardized math tests and took fewer math courses in high school, is closing. Another triumph is in sports, with record numbers of girls now playing on organized teams. While biases remain, the push for gender equity has clearly benefited girls and dispelled old-fashioned notions about girls' aptitude being lower than boys' in these areas.

But boys have not fared as well. Only recently have educators begun to recognize ways that boys are shortchanged at school. Boys as a group get lower grades than girls. They're also more likely to be left back and to drop out. Many researchers think that boys' low achievement is due, at least in part, to biases against boys. From the time they start school, boys are reprimanded more often than girls for not paying attention or for misbehaving. By the middle of elementary school, boys come to feel that teachers don't like them as much as they like girls. Boys are also overdiagnosed with learning disabilities because teachers often mistake their immature behavior for dyslexia and other learning problems. All this negative labeling early on is thought to drag down the self-esteem of many boys and with it, their will to strive.

But it's a mistake to blame gender bias for every test in which girls outperform boys, or vice versa. Researchers are coming to the view that boys and girls really do enter schools with different strengths and weaknesses. Girls are better able to sit still and pay attention, and they misbehave less than boys do. Many teachers and researchers think that girls also have an easier time learning to read. Though, contrary to widespread belief, girls don't have appreciably lower rates of reading disabilities than boys, they do appear to have less trouble overcoming them. On the other hand, boys consistently do better on intelligence tests of certain spatial skills, notably navigation and mental rotation, the ability to imagine the way a three-dimensional object looks from all angles. Mental rotation is related to an aptitude for math.

These gender differences seem to be partly biological. Males' superior ability in navigation and mental rotation has been associated with males' higher androgen levels. These "male" hormones may affect brain development in ways that favor these spatial skills. Other gender differences in the brain also seem significant. Girls' brains mature faster than boys', which is thought to explain why girls in the lower grades can sit still and concentrate better. Girls also have more brain cells devoted to language than boys do, which is probably an asset in learning to read and write.

But, as the saying goes, it's not where you begin but where you end up that's most important. And biological gender differences seem to have far less influence on where a child ends up than his or her experiences. Girls who have ample opportunity to explore and run around—even if it's within the protected limits of their own backyards or the local park—have better spatial skills than those who don't. Supportive teachers and parents help sustain girls' confidence in their ability to continue with math. They also inspire boys to read and write.

One of the two boys mentioned at the beginning of the chapter, whose meager output of words betrayed his struggle with the writing process, blossomed into one of the cleverest writers in his class. His second-grade teacher had the class keep a journal and write about whatever they wanted to. She also selected several books with engaging male characters to fire boys up for reading. His fourth-grade teacher—a man—also emphasized reading and writing in a way that inspired the students and made them think these subjects were cool. By the fourth grade, this boy was boasting to his friends that he reads every night before bed and talking about his writing assignments with the same fervor that he talked about sports.

SUGGESTIONS FOR PARENTS

Parents need to be advocates for their sons and daughters to prevent them from being shortchanged in their education. This means not only being alert to possible gender biases at school and at home, but giving children exposure to a broad range of experiences that can spark their interest in a range of subjects. Here are some recommendations from teachers and researchers who study gender issues in education, including advice that they followed as parents.

Cultivate your daughter's spatial skills.   Girls' performance in two key spatial tasks is consistently lower than boys', but one reason is that the have less experience with toys and activities that build spatial skills. "Several studies suggest that children's spatial skills are related to practice, training, and experience with toys that might provide opportunities to notice spatial principles," writes psychologist Carol Beal in her book, *Boys and Girls: The Development of Gender Roles*. Such experiences needn't be confined to building with blocks and playing baseball, she said. Playing with nesting cups, riding bikes, and playing soccer use spatial skills, too. Females' performance on spatial reasoning tests has improved over the past two generations, and Beal said that girls' greater involvement in sports and other physical activities may be partly responsible.

Read to Your Child Daily.   This is good all-round parenting advice, of course. Children who are read to every day from the time they're babies have an easier time than other children do learning how to read, according to research financed by the National Institutes of Health (NIH). They do so because by the time they start school, they've had years of practice with the building blocks of reading: connecting the letters and words with the sounds that they make. This practice may be especially important for boys, since boys as a group don't read as well as girls at all grade levels.

Find Books with Strong Male Characters.   Some researchers think that one reason boys don't read as much as girls do is that the books they read at school are too girlish. But giving boys books with engaging male characters, or nonfiction books and magazines on sports and other subjects they like, can make a big difference. Many a boy who professed to hate reading eagerly devoured the 300-plus-page "Harry Potter" books, the phenomenally popular fantasy series about a boy and his friends at a school for wizards. Books like these have the potential to improve boys' reading ability, which tends to be weaker than girls', because the more they read, the better they get at it.

Leave Gender Out of the Classroom.   By the end of elementary school, many children see math as a boys' subject and language arts as a girls' subject. They do so because many parents and teachers still expect boys to do better at math and girls to do better at language arts, and children pick up on these attitudes. Research shows that these expectations become self-fulfilling prophecies. Girls come to think of themselves as inferior math students, even if they do well at math, and the same is true for boys and language arts. Subtle remarks can have this effect. When mothers say things like, "I was bad at math," their daughters may think that math is especially tough for girls and then dislike math or stop trying to do well at it. That message is also driven home if Dad's the one who's pressed into service to help with the math homework. Hold your sons and daughters to high standards in all subjects, and if they're struggling with a subject, give them extra help.

Talk Up the Importance of Hard Work. The familiar gender biases about who's good at what subjects may be reinforced by sweeping generalizations about gender differences found in the brain, especially claims that these differences show that girls are fundamentally better at language-related subjects and boys at math. Children may find "proof" of these claims in their own observations. A girl who sees a boy in her class solve math problems effortlessly may point to him as evidence that boys are natural-born math whizzes. A boy who's awed by a girl's wonderful short story may assume that girls have a gift for writing. But where achievement is concerned, experts say that old-fashioned practice and effort are still what count the most. Let your children know that there's no shame in working hard and that it's a requirement in many subjects as they become more advanced.

Boost Your Daughter's Math Skills. Girls are as good as boys at adding, subtracting, multiplying, and dividing, but research suggests that there's one kind of math problem that trips many girls up—algebra word problems that involve comparing two quantities. Here's a simple example: "Amy has 2 candies. She has 1 candy less than Mary. How many candies does Mary have?" David Geary, a psychologist who has studied gender differences in math performance, said that more girls than boys get this kind of problem wrong because they have more trouble mentally diagramming the problem. So they mistakenly think that Mary has less candy than Amy.

The difference may not be enough to affect every girl's grades and SAT scores, but if your daughter is struggling with algebra word problems, Geary said that there's a simple way to help. Have your daughter diagram the problem on paper. In the case of the Amy and Mary problem, she'd write $X - 1 = 2$. When girls diagram algebra word problems on paper, they get more of them right, but when boys do so, their performance is unaffected.

Help Your Daughter Like Math and Science. Although girls' long-standing lag behind boys in both math and science has diminished, surveys show that girls still don't like these subjects very much. Research suggests that the reason is that girls have less experience outside the classroom with activities related to math and science—things like building transistor radios, playing with chemistry sets, and even more mundane activities like changing flat bicycle tires. "Tinkering around at home helps kids understand the utility and excitement of math and science," said Patricia Campbell, an educational consultant who has done research on ways to help interest girls in math.

To get girls on a more equal footing with boys in these areas, Campbell said that parents should encourage girls to do more of this tinkering for fun. This means more than just buying your daughter a chemistry set and hoping she'll love it. Parents' stories about their daughters rejecting chemistry sets are almost as legion as their stories about their sons rejecting dolls. Campbell said that the best way to interest girls in math and science is to do math- and science-related activities with them.

Know the Signs of Reading Disabilities.   Reading disabilities, the most common learning disabilities, are overdiagnosed in boys and underdiagnosed in girls. The reason is that boys tend to be wilder and more restless in class than girls, and their misbehavior during reading time in the early grades is often misinterpreted as a reading disorder. In any event, research has found that by the time a problem is diagnosed, girls with a reading disability are more severely impaired than boys.

It's important to diagnose reading disabilities early. Children with reading problems have a 95 percent chance of reading normally if they get extra help by the first or second grade, but just a 25 percent chance if they don't get it until the third grade. Research sponsored by NIH has found a simple test for predicting if a child will develop a reading disability. All that a parent or teacher has to do is sit with the child while he or she reads and notice how well the child sounds out words. If the child still has a lot of trouble breaking down most words into sounds by the beginning of the first grade, he or she needs extra help learning to read. This help should be one-on-one instruction in phonics (connecting letters with sounds) and phoneme awareness (hearing the sound components of spoken words) everyday at school and at home. NIH researchers say that all schools should give students this informal test, but if they don't, parents should and then tell the teacher if there's a problem.

Keep Recess at Your Child's School.   Many school districts are reducing or even eliminating recess in an effort to raise academic standards and lower injury rates and insurance liability.

But the trend can end up doing more harm than good, especially to boys. Boys have a harder time than girls sitting still and concentrating on schoolwork, and researchers have found that many boys who don't get a break to get up and move around often end up venting their frustration by acting out in class. Boys who misbehave are often pegged as having conduct disorders or learning disabilities, which lowers their self-esteem and sets them up for failure in school.

Make Sure Your Daughter Participates in Class. By the time their daughters reach the fourth grade, many parents hear the same complaint from the teachers: Your daughter doesn't raise her hand enough. One reason why girls don't participate as much as boys is that boys tend to shout out the answers, whether they know them or not. The other is that teachers, often without meaning to, give boys more attention. If the teacher said that your daughter isn't speaking up in class, ask your daughter why and what would help her want to participate more. If she said she'd feel more comfortable sitting in the front of the class, ask the teacher to switch her seat and call on her more often. If she said that the boys shout out the answers, tell the teacher. Keep checking in with your daughter and her teacher to make sure that she's getting equal time in class discussions.

Be Alert to Boy Bashing. Much of the extra attention boys get in class is negative and so, by the fourth grade, boys as well as girls think teachers like girls best, according to a recent survey of elementary school students. Students see teachers reprimanding and punishing boys more often than girls. Boys do misbehave more, and children who misbehave deserve to be punished. But often when a group of students act up, the teacher doesn't really know who's responsible. If the teacher or the monitors in the lunchroom or at recess single out mainly boys in these situations—and especially if your son thinks he's being unfairly accused—talk to the principal. Ideally, raising the possibility of a bias against boys will help the staff redouble its efforts to identify the students who really are misbehaving and not to assume guilt by association.

Get Your Daughter Involved in Sports. Boys have plenty of encouragement from their peers to play on a team or take sports classes, but girls may need it from their parents. Girls reap many benefits from participating in sports. The most obvious one is physical fitness—promoting lifelong good health habits, strengthening the heart, and controlling weight. But there are emotional and intellectual advantages, too. Girls who are involved in sports have lower rates of depression than do other girls. They may also have better spatial skills, which relate to mathematical skills. They get better grades. And they're more likely to become leaders. A 1997 report by the National Coalition for Girls and Women in Education found that 80 percent of the women who held managerial jobs in Fortune 500 companies played sports. "The link between sports and leadership for girls undoubtedly derives in part from the unique capacities for school sports to prompt students and adults to question their own assumptions about gender," noted a 1998 report on gender gaps in education by the AAUW.

There's an advantage to getting your daughter involved in sports early, since research shows that girls who don't participate in sports by the time they're 10 have just a 10 percent chance of being athletic when they're 25.

Fight Gender Bias in Sports. Girls have more opportunity to play organized sports now than ever before, but they continue to face discrimination. On co-ed teams, some coaches still let boys get away with refusing to pass balls to girls and criticizing girls' performance, according to the AAUW. With regard to single-sex teams, boy's teams often get better coaches and equipment, and when field space is limited, the boy's teams tend to get priority. If such biases affect your daughter, talk to her coach. If the coach is unresponsive or is part of the problem, take up the issue with the administrator of the sports association in question. If the bias occurs on a school team, go to the school administrators. Sex discrimination in school sports is against federal law, Title IX of the Education Amendments.

Help Your Daughter Stay in Sports.   More girls than boys drop out of sports. Gender bias is one reason—girls get tired of being sidelined while the boys get all the action on the field. But other reasons are more personal, notes Melissa Shafer of Girls Inc., an advocacy group. Even today some girls consider competitive sports unfeminine, or they just don't like to compete. There's a domino effect: As more girls leave organized sports, more of those who remain think about leaving.

There's no one-size-fits-all solution. Parents have to do what seems right for their daughters, with the goal of helping them stay physically active in some way. Jacquelynne Eccles, of the University of Michigan, recalls her daughter dropping out of team sports because there were too few girls playing. Eccles recommends that parents today do what she thinks might have helped her daughter stay with team sports: Talk to the parents of her daughter's friends and persuade them to sign their daughters up for a team. "It's hard for girls to stay with sports unless there are enough other girls on a team," she said.

Elin Waring of New York City tried to encourage her daughter to join various athletic teams, but the 10 year old just wasn't interested. Though she loved to swim, she refused to join the swim team because she didn't like to compete. So Elin has helped her daughter stay physically active in noncompetitive ways. First, she joined several other parents in persuading her daughter's school to offer dance as part of physical education. Second, she makes sure that her daughter gets into a pool on a regular basis, not to compete but to take lessons to refine her skills.

5

Boys, Girls, and Health

Gender Differences in Symptoms and Illnesses

FEMALE TROUBLES, MALE TROUBLES

It's no news that some health problems are more common in boys and that others are more common in girls. Eating disorders are considered largely female illnesses, for example, whereas autism is more prevalent in males. But lately doctors have discovered that other conditions, long thought to know no gender, affect males and females in different numbers or in different ways.

It's not that a band of medical detectives went looking for sex differences in seemingly sexless problems. But differences showed up and kept showing up so regularly that they couldn't be ignored. For example, asthma rates across the country have doubled in the past two decades, and about one-third of the sufferers are children, but for some reason asthma is more common in boys than in girls before adolescence and more common in girls during and after adolescence. Sports injuries are increasing because more children are playing sports, but isn't it odd that so many girls need knee surgery? Sex differences have also been found in autoimmune diseases, diabetes, sensitivity to pain, and the risk of and survival rates for certain cancers.

Why? In some cases, the explanation is straightforward. For example, Duchennes muscular dystrophy, a degenerative muscle disorder that affects only boys, is linked to a defective gene on the X chromosome. It can be inherited only by boys from their mothers, since boys inherit their single X chromosome from their mothers. But for most of the illnesses with a gender difference, there is no clear answer. There's not even a common denominator.

Take cancer, for instance. Smoking is bad for everybody, but the odds of a woman developing lung cancer are as much as 70 percent higher than for a man, even if they smoked the same number of cigarettes for the same number of years. Researchers think that females may be more sensitive to the carcinogens in cigarettes. In any case, females' high lung cancer risk is especially disturbing, given that girls now take up smoking in equal numbers to boys but have a harder time quitting.

Whatever it is that makes females more vulnerable to lung cancer doesn't make them more vulnerable to all forms of cancer. More boys than girls get acute lymphocytic leukemia, the most common childhood cancer, and the girls who do get it have slightly better odds of survival. This gender difference is well known among cancer specialists, but it's only in the past few years that they have started asking why—and how they can use this information to save children's lives. Now some doctors are looking for genes and other possible reasons why lymphocytic leukemia is tougher for boys to beat, and they're considering whether boys with the disease should get more aggressive therapy.

For the most part, doctors are still in what may be called the box-score stage, gathering statistics on which problems are more common or severe in boys versus girls. But their growing list of statistics has given rise to a new field of medical research—gender-based medicine, the study of how and why sex matters in diseases and disabilities. The effort has already turned up tantalizing clues that help explain why boys and girls are predisposed to different ailments.

One of the most intriguing clues is that girls have stronger immune systems, which is a good thing for fighting off infections, but this strength can be a weakness when it comes to chronic diseases like lupus, which are caused by runaway immune- system activity. Anatomical differences are important, too. Girls have weaker knees, which is one reason why girls are at a higher risk of knee injuries. Sex differences in the brain may explain why boys suffer more from some kinds of brain disorders, such as autism and attention deficit-hyperactivity disorder, and why girls are more susceptible to others, like anxiety.

But gender differences in health aren't just a matter of biology. Boys' and girls' experiences count, too, and experience works with biology to put boys and girls at risk of different problems. A prime example is knee injuries. In addition to a fundamental weakness in their knees (nature), girls' higher risk of knee injuries is now seen as a result of their unequal access to sports training programs that would help them strengthen the muscles and ligaments around their knees (nurture).

One day, gender-based medicine may lead to different ways of preventing and treating illnesses in girls and boys. At least, that's the goal. But for the time being, just being aware that there are differences can be beneficial because it can lead to earlier detection of disorders that often go unrecognized in boys and others that go unrecognized in girls. What follows is a description of health problems that affect boys and girls in unequal numbers and the reasons, or suspected reasons, why. At the end of the chapter are suggestions on how to protect your daughters and sons from some of these conditions and how to recognize the symptoms of the others so that you can catch them early and minimize their damage.

ACCIDENTS

George has an open face and a zest for adventure. As a toddler, he'd climb out of his crib and wander downstairs early in the morning while his parents were still sleeping. Once, he fell downstairs and needed stitches. At 5, he'd walk on the brick wall framing the front stoop of his Brooklyn row house, balancing himself as if on a tightrope. One day, he lost his balance and broke his arm. None of his injuries kept George from flirting with danger again. By the time he entered kindergarten, he'd been to the hospital once for every year of his life.

Throughout childhood, far more boys than girls are injured as a result of accidents, like falling down stairs or off the monkey bars or having other mishaps. Among 1 to 4 year olds, about 11 out of every 100,000 boys die of accidents (other than automobile accidents, which are beyond their control), compared with about 7 out of 100,000 girls that age. In the 5- to 14 age group, the rate of accidental deaths is about 5 in 100,000 boys, twice as high as it is for girls.

Boys get injured more because practically from the time they can walk, they take more risks, which inevitably lead to more accidents. Some of this devil-may-care behavior can be chalked up to impulsiveness. Young boys as a group have less self-control than girls as a group. And among schoolchildren, boys are more prone to attention deficit-hyperactivity disorder, a developmental disability characterized in part by impulsiveness. But impulsiveness doesn't fully explain why boys are more willing to do things like jump off the top of a slide or, like George, see how far they can walk along a narrow brick wall. The difference in risk-taking behavior comes down to a difference in mindset.

In her ongoing research on children's risk-taking behavior, Barbara Morrongiello, a psychologist at the University of Guelph in Canada, has found three key differences between boys and girls. For one thing, boys don't consider given activities to be as dangerous as girls do. When Morrongiello asked 6- to 10 year olds to rate how risky certain activities were—climbing a playground structure barefoot while holding a soda can in one hand, for example—the boys saw less potential danger than the girls did. Second, even when they acknowledged a degree of risk in an activity, the boys saw less chance of being injured. They didn't think *they'll* be the ones to get hurt, or they thought that if they did get hurt, the injury wouldn't be bad. Finally, the boys were more fatalistic about injuries. When the children were asked whose fault it would be if they were injured doing something risky, the boys were more likely to say it was "bad luck," whereas the girls were more likely to blame themselves.

As toddlers, girls and boys can't put their attitudes toward risk into words, of course, but they reveal them in their actions. Morrongiello set up an experiment with 2- to 3 year olds and their mothers in which they went into a room with pretend versions of dangerous objects, like scissors, that young children are routinely told not to touch. Then Morrongiello videotaped the children's reactions to these well-known hazards. "The boys and girls were equally interested in them," she said. "But the girls would go over and point to them or call their mothers' attention to them. The boys would go over and touch them before the mothers had a chance to see what they were doing."

If anything good comes of this sort of reckless behavior in real life, parents may logically assume it's that once children get injured, they'll learn their lesson and be more careful the next time. But while this happens with some children, Morrongiello said, it doesn't happen with the hard-core risk takers: "One of the biggest risk factors for a child showing up in an emergency room with an injury related to risky behavior is that the child has had the injury before." In her study of toddlers, the children who went right over and touched the dangerous objects were the ones who, in their brief lives, already had a history of accidental injuries.

Morrongiello and other researchers think that there must be biological differences that drive boys to take more risks than girls. In his groundbreaking studies of temperamental traits in children, Jerome Kagan, of Harvard, found that boys were less inhibited and fearful than girls and that inhibited children, as one might imagine, took fewer risks. He also found that the inhibited children had more biological indicators of stress, like higher levels of cortisol, a stress hormone, as well as higher heart rates and greater muscle tension.

In addition, Kagan found that brain activity was somewhat different in the inhibited and the uninhibited children. When electrical activity in their brains was measured in a laboratory, the inhibited children showed more activity in the right frontal cortex and the uninhibited children showed more activity in the left frontal cortex. It could be that the two hemispheres of the frontal cortex are the wellsprings of two opposite temperaments: the right hemisphere for inhibition and the left for risk taking. In support of this theory, Kagan noted that adults who consider themselves extroverts (and probably are willing to take some chances) show the left-dominant pattern, whereas adults who describe themselves as being extremely shy or anxious (too scared to take risks) show the right-dominant pattern in the frontal cortex.

But neither Kagan nor Morrongiello thinks that brain activity entirely explains the gender difference in risk-taking behavior. Biology may predispose a child to take or avoid risks, but whether or not that predisposition becomes destiny depends on how the child is raised. In her work, Morrongiello has observed that fathers and mothers reinforce a penchant for risk taking in their sons by encouraging them to meet physical challenges, saying things like, "Come on, you can do it." At first, in toddlerhood, these challenges may be climbing on new structures at the playground, but as the boys get older they may involve recreational activities like Rollerblading or going out for the football team.

Of course, many parents also support their daughters' pursuit of physical challenges, but Morrongiello has found that they tend to pepper their support with what she calls "vulnerability statements." "Girls who are doing the same things as boys on the playground are getting more cautions like, 'Be careful,' 'You could get hurt,' and 'You could crack your head open,'" she said. "Parents are more likely to grab and help their daughters do something. This tendency sends subtle cues to their daughters that they're more vulnerable to injury."

Do girls need more encouragement just to go for it? Do boys need more words of caution? There's no formula to help children achieve the ideal balance of adventurousness and wariness, whatever that balance may be. But there are ways to help prevent injuries by reducing risk-taking behavior. The just-say-no approach doesn't work, Morrongiello said. Rather, the idea is to help children make the connection between a risk and its consequences. Morrongiello advises starting young. She's trying to teach her 1-year-old son not to touch dangerous objects like hot coffee cups. But instead of saying, "Don't touch," she simply says, "Hot." Now her son points to coffee cups and says, "Hot," and stays away from them.

A lot of parents use strategies like Morrongiello's, but do they help keep children out of harm's way in the long run? Morrongiello has indirect evidence that they do. She ran a program in four elementary schools in Toronto that aimed to reduce risky behavior that can cause severe head injuries, such as riding a bike without a helmet and diving into a shallow lake. But instead of lecturing the students, who were 8- to 10 year olds, Morrongiello set up activities that allowed the children to experience how hard it would be to live with disabilities associated with head injuries, like blindness, deafness, and the loss of function in an arm or leg. One activity was for the children to try to use one hand to do such everyday tasks as tying their shoes and zipping their knapsacks. They came to see how hard it was to do these basic things, how much help they'd need, and how much extra time they would have to allot just to get to class each day. Four months later, the children reported engaging in less risky behavior than they did before the program began.

ANXIETY

Jessica started out a happy, sociable child. Although she had severe food allergies, which meant that she had to bring her own wheat-free, dairy-free cake when she went to birthday parties, she seemed to take this adjustment in stride. All that changed when she was 6. Her family moved to another state, and Jessica and her older sister were sad to say good-bye to their friends. But Jessica's sister made a smooth transition to her new school and formed new friendships, and Jessica didn't.

It's not that the children in Jessica's new class were unfriendly. Several girls invited her over for play dates and so forth. But Jessica didn't want to get to know them. She didn't like her new school. Her parents assumed that she'd adjust with time, but as time passed, things got worse. When she was in school, she would cry to go home. At home she was afraid to be alone in a room. She frequently complained of stomachaches and headaches. Jessica's parents took her to a psychiatrist, who diagnosed anxiety disorder.

Did the family's move somehow cause Jessica's extreme, disabling fearfulness? Was her anxiety a delayed emotional reaction to her life-threatening allergies? These are the questions that haunt Jessica's parents, even though they know that many children become anxious after moving to a new house or suffering from a chronic illness, but most don't develop an anxiety *disorder*. Why Jessica?

Anxiety has long been seen as a female problem. Most of the 2 percent to 7 percent of children with an anxiety disorder are girls, and most of the adults are women. For years, social scientists debated whether females are fundamentally more anxiety prone or whether more of them are identified with anxiety because of other factors. For example, girls and women more readily admit to feeling anxious. To help settle the debate, psychologists at the Oregon Research Institute and Stanford University recently interviewed about two thousand college students about their history of anxiety disorders and anxiety-related symptoms. They eliminated the girls with psychosocial problems associated with anxiety, like low self-esteem and conflicts at home. But they still reached the age-old conclusion: Females as a group really are more anxiety prone.

Beginning at age 6, the girls in the study were twice as likely as the boys to be affected, and anxiety remained more common among females as they grew up. The study didn't dismiss the role of social problems, like low self-esteem, in putting girls at a higher risk of anxiety than boys. But it did conclude that there may be genetic or other biological factors that predispose girls to anxiety. No one knows what those factors might be in a young girl—no anxiety gene has been found. But researchers think that the factors probably trigger imbalances of brain chemicals like serotonin that affect mood and hormones released under stress. Such imbalances play a role in depression, and depression is so closely linked with anxiety that children and adults with one often have the other, although not necessarily at the same time. Girls like Jessica who develop anxiety at a young age are considered to be at an especially high risk for depression in their teens.

Recognizing anxiety symptoms early is the key to preventing anxiety from leading to depression or snowballing to the point that a child can't make friends and function in school, as happened with Jessica. "A child who has a high level of anxiety about separating from a parent or going to school is not OK— this portends a negative future," said Susan Nolen-Hoeksema, a psychologist at the University of Michigan who studies sex differences in anxiety and depression. Nolen-Hoeksema says that when a child's anxiety is caught early enough, it can often be helped by two kinds of behavioral therapy. One is relaxation therapy, in which the child is trained to relax her body in situations that make her anxious. The other is desensitization, in which she spends progressively more time in these situations.

Let's say your child is afraid to go to school because she thinks something bad will happen to you when she's gone. The strategy is to have the child spend more time each day in school until she spends a full day there. When you say good-bye, you should leave at the appointed time each day, even if the child is crying. To help get over her fear at the time of separation, she should do her relaxation exercises. Over a period of weeks or months, if the therapy works, the child will gradually become desensitized to the experience of separating from you. If behavioral therapy doesn't work or if a child has severe anxiety, antianxiety medication may be needed to control her symptoms to the point that she can join her peers and enjoy childhood activities.

ASTHMA

Eight-year-old Jeff and his 6-year-old sister, Laura, both have asthma, periodic bouts of shortness of breath and wheezing. Although they don't have to cut back on bike riding, baseball, or any other physical activities, they do have to take precautions in the form of annual flu shots and occasional medication to prevent life-threatening asthma attacks. Both children hope that one day they will outgrow their asthma, but Jeff stands a far greater chance of getting his wish simply because he is a boy.

Asthma starts out worse in boys—from birth to age 10, boys are twice as likely to be hospitalized with an asthma attack. For the time being, Jeff's asthma is worse than Laura's. But after about age 10, boys usually get better and girls get worse. By age 11, girls are admitted to hospital emergency rooms with asthma attacks more often than boys. By age 13 and thereafter, asthma is such an overwhelmingly female illness that girls and women account for 75 percent of the asthma patients rushed to emergency rooms.

Emil Skobeloff, an emergency room physician and leading researcher on gender differences in asthma, has seen this general pattern in his patients, as well as in his own children. His two sons, aged 4 and 10, and his 7-year-old daughter all have asthma. "The big guy's asthma has gotten better over the years," Skobeloff said. But his daughter's hasn't. "It really worries me what may happen to her as she gets into puberty."

Estrogen seems to make girls more vulnerable to asthma as they approach their teens. It's not high estrogen per se but, rather, the ups and downs of estrogen during the menstrual cycle that appear to trigger asthma attacks. Skobeloff has documented a fourfold increase in the number of teenage girls and women treated in emergency rooms for asthma attacks just before or during their periods, when estrogen plummets from its monthly peak. He thinks that the rapid drop in estrogen somehow makes the airways more reactive. What this means is that common triggers of asthma, like cold air or dust, that may not bother a particular girl or woman at other times of the month can induce an asthma attack on days 26 to 31 of the menstrual cycle. If estrogen is as important a factor as Skobeloff's research suggests, then it makes sense that girls' asthma would get worse after around age 10, since this is the time when their estrogen levels surge.

There are other reasons to think that estrogen affects the airways. When animals are given increased estradiol, a form of estrogen, they produce more mucus and their lung cells show unusual changes. And when women with asthma are pregnant, their symptoms get worse if the fetus is a girl but stay the same or improve if it's a boy. There's more estrogen in the womb when the developing baby is a girl. How and why estrogen affects asthma remains a mystery, but chances are it's not the only sex-related factor, since boys are more susceptible to asthma than girls in the early years. The reason for the increased risk in young boys is one of the many puzzles in gender-based medicine.

Until more is known about gender differences in asthma, Skobeloff doesn't see a reason for parents to treat their sons and daughters differently when they have asthma. What's most important is for children to take their asthma medicine as prescribed and for parents to know what to do during an asthma attack. First, give the child a dose of oral steroids to open the airways. If the child gets worse, call 911. "Don't drive an asthmatic person having an attack to the E.R.," Skobeloff said. Your child can get lifesaving treatment in the back of an ambulance that he or she can't get in the back or your car.

ATTENTION DEFICIT-HYPERACTIVITY DISORDER

In the first grade, when Kristal was supposed to be learning to read, she was still struggling to learn the sequence of the alphabet. Her father would try to help her, and she'd finally get it, but by the next day at school she'd be confused again about the order of the letters. Kristal's parents could see that she had trouble concentrating, and they brought this problem up with the teacher, but the teacher passed it off as the immaturity typical of a 6 year old. The teacher thought Kristal's difficulty learning the alphabet was caused by a learning disability and recommended a special education class at school.

The special ed class didn't help. Kristal still struggled to learn—she couldn't focus on any task for very long. "If she had trouble doing a work sheet, she'd just start coloring on a piece of paper," her mother said. "Or if the door to the classroom was open and the principal passed by, she'd run out and say Hi to the principal." Convinced that Kristal's problem was something more than a learning disability, Kristal's parents asked the school psychologist to evaluate her. The diagnosis was attention deficit-hyperactivity disorder (ADHD), a developmental problem that impairs attention; interferes with learning; and often causes wild, impulsive behavior.

Kristal's teacher probably would have suspected the problem

if Kristal were a boy, since ADHD is more common in boys. Just how much more common is a matter of dispute, however. ADHD is diagnosed in three- to five times as many boys as girls, but psychiatrists now think the gender difference, although real, isn't quite so great. They think that the disorder is overdiagnosed in boys and underdiagnosed in girls because boys' natural rambunctiousness and high energy are sometimes mistakenly seen as pathological.

Still, it's easy to see why ADHD would be noticed more in boys. The symptoms are different in boys than they are in girls, and boys with ADHD have more of the symptoms that parents, teachers, and doctors commonly associated with the disorder: They're hyperactive in addition to being inattentive and impulsive. Girls with ADHD, on the other hand, usually aren't hyperactive. Their main problems are the ones Kristal had— trouble paying attention, distractibility, and difficulty learning.

The longer ADHD goes untreated, the more it can interfere with a child's ability to learn. And since girls tend to be diagnosed with ADHD later than boys, they have more serious learning problems and attention deficits than do boys. "Given that their baseline of hyperactivity and impulsivity is lower than boys, they may have to exhibit more severe symptoms in order to be picked up as abnormal," said Monique Ernst, an ADHD researcher at the NIH. But Ernst doesn't think that gender bias in diagnosis is solely to blame. "There may be some protective factor in girls that makes them exhibit symptoms only when the condition is severe," she said.

No doubt, the clues to what that protective factor may be and why ADHD is more common in boys lie within boys' and girls' brains. Recently, scientists have been peering inside the brains of children with ADHD to compare them to the brains of healthy children without the disorder. And the brains look different.

Children with ADHD have smaller brains and significantly less gray matter, a type of nerve cells, than other children. The lack of gray matter is most noticeable in the right frontal lobe, which controls motor activity, attention, and high-level thinking. Using brain-imaging technology called functional magnetic resonance imaging, which allows scientists to watch the brain at work, Stewart Mostofsky, a neurologist at the Kennedy Krieger Insutute at Johns Hopkins School of Medicine in Baltimore, has seen the inattentiveness characteristic of ADHD. He found that when performing a task that requires attentiveness, the right hemisphere's reaction time is slower in boys with ADHD than it is in other boys. The same difference in the landscape of the brain is seen in girls with and without ADHD, according to research at NIH.

It could be that the brain abnormalities associated with ADHD are more likely to cause symptoms in boys, for the same reason that a stroke is more debilitating to men than to women, notes Mostofsky. Females' ability to use both sides of their brains for certain tasks makes them better equipped to compensate when they suffer damage to one side. Women with stroke damage that leaves them unable to speak stand a greater chance of being able to talk again than do men with the same damage.

Other factors could also put boys at a higher risk of ADHD. Difficult conditions before and after birth seem to contribute to the condition. These include problems during pregnancy and delivery, marital discord, and low socioeconomic status. Recall that the odds of a long, arduous childbirth are the greatest when the baby is a boy. And there's some evidence that boys' cognitive abilities suffer more than girls' as a result of malnutrition, as well as a lack of love and attention in early childhood. ADHD may be related to such deprivation.

In any event, it's important to diagnose ADHD soon after a

child starts school, otherwise it can lead to school failure and social problems, like difficulty in making friends. Parents need to be especially alert to the signs in their daughters because, as Kristal's parents discovered, teachers aren't. Boys and girls with ADHD respond equally well to the standard treatments, which include psychotherapy, private tutoring to help children concentrate better on their schoolwork, and drug therapy with such stimulants as Ritalin.

AUTOIMMUNE DISEASES

Ann was well acquainted with the scrapes and muscular aches of sports injuries during her active childhood. But when she was 17, she had a strange symptom. Both of her ankles hurt and felt stiff. At first, Ann thought she had sprained them, but she soon realized that that was unlikely since she hadn't twisted or injured them in any way. So she did what many teenagers do when faced with a problem that makes no sense: She tried to ignore it.

But Ann couldn't ignore the discomfort because it got worse. The pain and stiffness traveled up her legs, then infiltrated her arms. Her doctor thought she had Lyme disease, a tick-borne infection that often causes joint pain and that is rampant around her home in New York's Hudson Valley. But the Lyme test was negative. As time passed, Ann's joint pain was so bad that she could hardly walk. She soon developed shortness of breath. Eventually, she was admitted to the hospital, where she was seen by a constellation of specialists—rheumatologists, cardiologists, and experts on infectious diseases. Many weeks and many tests later came the diagnosis: Mixed connective tissue disorder.

Mixed connective tissue disorder is one of many autoimmune diseases, incurable illnesses in which a person's immune

system goes awry and attacks its own body as if it were an invad-
ing germ. Other autoimmune diseases include multiple sclero-
sis, rheumatoid arthritis, and systemic lupus erythematosus.
The immune system's assault damages muscles, tendons, bones,
and sometimes vital organs like the heart and kidneys. About
three-quarters of the 8.5 million people in the United States
who have autoimmune diseases are female.

Why are girls and women more prone to autoimmune diseases? The short answer is that their immune systems are somewhat stronger than males'. After a vaccination, girls produce
more antibodies than do boys. As far as anyone can tell, the
extra immune-system cells don't make enough of a difference to
give girls more protection from infections— girls get as many of
them as boys. But the difference may be just enough to put girls
over the edge should their immune systems spin out of control.

Girls' robust immune systems seem to be related to sex hormones. Estrogen, a sex hormone that is higher in females,
enhances specific immune functions, whereas testosterone,
which is higher in males, suppresses them. It's no surprise, then,
that the gender difference in autoimmune diseases is greatest
after puberty and during the childbearing years, when the gender difference in the levels of the sex hormones is the greatest.
However, autoimmune disorders can strike children as young as
5, and no matter what the child's age, the disorders are still more
common in girls.

Scientists don't know what makes a person's immune system
turn on the body. "It looks like there's an orchestration of
events," said Caroline Whitacre, an immunologist at Ohio State
University and a member of a national task force of researchers
who are investigating the reasons for gender differences in
autoimmune diseases. Whitacre said that there's no support for
the popular notion that vaccinations trigger autoimmune dis-

eases, but it does seem that the first event is probably a viral infection in childhood. The infection could be something as commonplace as a cold. The symptoms go away, but for some reason the virus hides out in the body and keeps stimulating the immune system.

The extra stimulation alone probably wouldn't be enough to put the immune system in reverse so that it destroys what it's supposed to protect. For that to happen, doctors think there have to be defects in the genes that are in charge of keeping the immune system on target. Evidence of a genetic component comes from studies showing that autoimmune disorders run in families and are more common among identical twins—who have identical genes—than among other siblings. Possible genes have been identified in laboratory mice.

Doctors don't know how to prevent autoimmune diseases, so for the time being the best thing parents can do is to be alert to the symptoms, especially in their daughters, and bring them to a doctor's attention. Without parents' help, doctors often dismiss the symptoms, since the symptoms are vague and come and go. Like Ann, many people have symptoms for months or even years before the cause is diagnosed. But the longer it takes to make a diagnosis and begin treatment, the greater the chance that the immune system will begin attacking a vital organ like the heart, putting the child's life at risk. Steroid medicine can relieve the pain and stiffness and slow the progress of the illness.

BED-WETTING

Paul is a star Little League player, a gifted student, and a popular 8 year old. Because his life is charmed in many ways, he's a bit of a wise guy. To the outside world, Paul has everything going for him. What no one other than his parents knows is that Paul rarely gets through the night without wetting his bed. Paul does everything he can to stay dry at night. He doesn't drink anything before bedtime. He goes to the bathroom before shutting out his light. But nothing works.

Paul may feel like he's the only child his age who still wets his bed, but about 15 percent to 20 percent of children over age 5 have the same problem, and boys outnumber girls by as much as 2 to 1. Bed-wetting isn't caused by an illness or a physical abnormality. In fact, about 15 percent of children outgrow the problem each year without any treatment, an indication that it's not really a disorder but, rather, a delay in maturation. So, it stands to reason that more boys would be affected, since boys mature more slowly in some respects than girls.

It seems that one of the delays that is central to bed-wetting involves the communication between the brain and the bladder. The cortex in the brain is supposed to signal the nerves and muscles around the bladder's sphincter to hold urine in until a person reaches the bathroom. Doctors think that cortex-to-bladder communication has to reach a certain level of development before a child can be toilet trained, and boys as a group are later to train than girls. Most bet-wetters don't have accidents during the day, although it's possible that the necessary nerve pathway is mature enough to alert them to go to the bathroom when they are awake but not to go the extra step and wake them up to go to the bathroom.

Other factors may keep boys from staying dry at night. Many bet-wetters don't have enough antidiuretic hormone, which is supposed to decrease urine production at night. Since the brain controls the release of hormones, boys' lag in brain development could explain the antidiuretic hormone deficiency. It may also be significant that boys' bladders are more complicated than girls'. Boys' bladders have several muscles involved in holding urine in, whereas girls' bladders have just one. It's possible that the more muscles that are involved, the more complex the process of brain-to-bladder communication is.

Bed-wetting is known to be genetic. One study found that in families in which both parents were bet-wetters, children faced a 77 percent chance of being bet-wetters, but when neither parent had the problem, children's chance is just 15 percent. Although a bed-wetting gene itself hasn't been found, a marker for it has. Some scientists think that the gene is responsible for excess urine production. Others think it may affect brain mechanisms that influence how deeply a child sleeps and how easily he or she can be awakened.

Emotional and psychological distress may also explain why most bet-wetters are boys. Many child development researchers think that during early elementary school, the time when bed-wetting is most common, boys struggle more than girls with any number of things: adjusting to school, learning to read, and coping with pressure from the other boys to be tough. There's no question that stressful problems like these are related to bed-wetting, said Marc Cendron, a pediatric urologist at Dartmouth-Hitchcock Medical Center in New Hampshire who treats bet-wetters. Cendron said that bed-wetting tends to be worse during times of stress, like divorce or the birth of a sibling, starting school, or on the night after a bad day in school.

Yet another reason why bed-wetting is more common in boys is that it seems to occur along with ADHD, which is also more common in boys. Though research has yet to explore the connection, Cendron said that he and other doctors who treat bet-wetters find that a lot of them also have ADHD and that doctors who treat ADHD find that a large share of their patients are bet-wetters.

Bed-wetting isn't harmful itself, but it can inflict psychological harm in a child by lowering his self-esteem. Some children end up feeling socially isolated by their fear of having sleepovers. Studies have found that bed-wetting sometimes leads to depression. Parents can help prevent such problems by being understanding and explaining to their children that bed-wetting isn't their fault and that they'll outgrow it eventually. If such assurance doesn't comfort the child or if he shows signs of psychological disturbance, Cendron said that parents should talk to their child's doctor about treatment options. One is a drug supplement of antidiuretic hormone. And there are devices that a child can wear to bed that sound an alarm when he begins to urinate. The purpose of the alarm is to condition the child to wake up when he needs to go to the bathroom.

DEPRESSION

Depression is so widely seen as a female illness that many parents expect their daughters to sulk and have angry outbursts, especially as they approach their teens. In fact, the earliest sign of puberty—preceding physical changes—is an increase in mood swings. The great attention paid to depression in girls is justified, given that the disorder is twice as common in teenage girls as in teenage boys.

But this statistic gives the false impression that boys don't get depressed, when the fact is that depression strikes boys and girls at different times and in different ways. Depression is more common in boys than in girls before the teenage years. And since 1.8 million preadolescent children are clinically depressed, the number of boys affected is not trivial. Depression becomes more common in both boys and girls as they get older and face more social and academic pressures, but the incidence rises faster in girls starting at about age 11.

Biology accounts for some of the gender difference in depression. People who are depressed have low levels of serotonin in the brain, a nervous system chemical that affects mood, and norepinephrine, a hormone released in response to stress. Girls tend to have unstable serotonin and norepinephrine levels around adolescence because their levels of estrogen and progesterone are in flux, and imbalances in these hormones cause imbalances in serotonin and norepinephrine.

But what about boys? These hormonal ups and downs don't explain why more boys than girls get depressed in elementary school. Nolen-Hoeksema thinks that as with some other problems, boys' vulnerability to depression is related to their lag in brain maturation. This lag may make it harder for young boys to control their emotions well enough to cope with difficult situations, such as divorce or other stressful events at home. Nolen-Hoeksema points to research showing that boys are more likely to suffer from emotional problems when their parents divorce. The lag in brain maturation is probably also related to bed-wetting, another problem that is more common in boys that can lead to depression.

But it takes more than slow brain maturation or fluctuating hormones to trigger clinical depression. Nolen-Hoeksema thinks that the different ways that boys and girls are treated plays a key role. In particular, the tendency of some parents and other adults as well as peers to urge boys to be tough can leave them vulnerable to depression, especially at times of crisis or trauma when they may need to talk about how they feel. With girls, the problem certainly isn't too little talk about feelings but rather too much. Girls are allowed—even encouraged—to ruminate over bad feelings, and rumination is associated with depression.

Nolen-Hoeksema and Joan Girgus, of Princeton University, recently surveyed 615 boys and girls aged 11 to 15 in the San Francisco Bay Area, asking them to rate how much they worried about a wide range of subjects, like school, getting along with parents, appearance, and friends. The girls worried more about nearly everything. There was one exception: The boys worried about more "sports and other activities." So, boys not only have fewer worries, but the things they worry about have less of an emotional kick. What causes deeper, more lasting anguish—losing a game or losing a friend?

Nolen-Hoeksema thinks that girls get into the habit of ruminating because they spend a lot of time mulling over their feelings with their mothers and their friends. Beginning when their children are infants, mothers talk more with their daughters than with their sons, and much of this talk is about emotions. The problem, Nolen-Hoeksema said, is that they devote too much time dwelling on negative feelings and not enough time talking about how to get beyond them.

Nolen-Hoeksema isn't saying that mothers bear the main responsibility for their daughters' rumination. She thinks that, to some extent, girls come by it naturally, perhaps because of a temperamental trait—fearfulness, for instance—that keeps them from letting go of distressing thoughts. She also thinks that girls are more given to rumination during adolescence, when the shake-up of hormones and brain chemicals can make them moody. And then, adolescent girls arguably have more of the sorts of experiences that lead to rumination and depression. Girls are twice as likely as boys to be sexually abused. One in five girls has been sexually or physically abused, and sexual abuse, understandably, often leads to depression.

In addition to the gender difference in the onset of depression, boys and girls have somewhat different symptoms. Girls have mainly "internalizing" symptoms, which means that they tend to become anxious or withdraw from other people. Depressed boys, on the other hand, have mainly "externalizing" symptoms like frequent misbehavior and getting into fights. As such, depression in boys looks a lot like ADHD, which isn't surprising since many boys with ADHD become depressed because of the trouble they have making friends, said Nolen-Hoeksema.

In other respects, boys and girls with depression are similar. They become extremely irritable. Their sleep pattern changes, so that they sleep either more or less than usual. Their schoolwork slides. They lose interest in activities that they used to enjoy. They spend more and more time alone. If you think your child is depressed, talk to a therapist who specializes in children. Effective treatments for childhood depression include cognitive-behavioral therapy, which helps children avoid negative thinking and improve their social skills, as well as antidepressants.

The sooner you get help, the better, Nolen-Hoeksema said. Early treatment can save a child's life. Depression is one of the biggest risk factors for childhood and teenage suicide, which has doubled since 1980 among 10- to 14 year olds. Girls talk more about committing suicide than boys do, but boys, in keeping with their tendency to act instead of stew, are more likely to go through with it.

DIABETES

Adult-onset diabetes was long thought to be just what its name suggests, a disease that comes on in adulthood. But in the past few years, doctors around the country have been surprised by a sudden surge in children as young as 7 with the disorder, which is characterized by abnormally high levels of sugar in the blood. Most of these children are girls.

In many cases, the girls go for months without even knowing that they're sick, since adult-onset diabetes causes only vague symptoms, such as lethargy. Doctors say that many girls are found to have daibetes when routine urine exams show high sugar levels. Other girls are found to have adult-onset diabetes after they have had a series of urinary tract infections, which become more common as blood sugar levels rise.

The reason why more children are getting adult-onset diabetes is that more children are overweight, and obesity interferes with the body's mechanism for controlling blood sugar. The number of obese children in the United States has climbed by 50 percent over the past decade, to 1 in 5 children. Nearly all the children with adult-onset diabetes are overweight. But the reason why about 60 percent to 70 percent of the children with adult-onset diabetes are girls is that obesity is more common in girls. Girls are less physically active than boys, especially as they enter their teens, and more girls suffer from binge-eating disorder, which is extreme overeating on a regular basis (see Eating Disorders, pages 224–27).

Unless their blood sugar is brought down to normal limits, children with adult-onset diabetes can develop devastating complications, such as blindness or kidney disease, in their twenties or earlier. To lower their blood sugar, doctors first recommend that the children exercise more and eat fewer high-fat foods and more fruits and vegetables. However, doctors say that few children can control the condition with diet and exercise alone. Most children also need to take medicine that increases their production of insulin, the hormone that controls blood sugar, and increases their body's sensitivity to insulin. But doctors think that if children spent less time watching TV or playing

Nintendo and more time running around in the park, fewer of them would get adult-onset diabetes.

EATING DISORDERS

One day, my daughter lifted her shirt, pinched the skin on her abdomen, and said she was fat. Her statement was surprising for two reasons. First, she wasn't fat. Second, she was barely out of diapers. How did she know, at age 3, what fat was? We didn't talk about "fat people" or complain about our weight. Did her preschool friends? In the two years since then, Sarah has said, "I'm fat," several times, apparently oblivious to her willowy frame. I wonder where this idea comes from and I worry where it will lead as she approaches the age when eating disorders become all too common in girls.

Certainly, one of the biggest risk factors for eating disorders is simply being female. Eighty-five to 95 percent of people with anorexia nervosa and bulimia nervosa are girls and women, as are 60 percent of those with binge-eating disorder. *Eating disorders* is a catchall term that encompasses all these problems, although the problems are not as separate as they may seem. As many as half the patients with anorexia also sometimes show signs of bulimia and binge-eating disorder.

Anorexia is compulsive and extreme dieting, an intense fear of gaining weight and a distorted perception of one's weight or size—a girl thinking that she's fat when she's pencil-thin. Nearly 20 percent of people with anorexia die of it, which means anorexia has the highest mortality rate of any mental illness. Bulimia is regular binge eating, followed by induced vomiting, purging, or fasting. Though less dangerous than anorexia, bulimia can also cause health problems, like fatigue and erosion of tooth enamel. Binge-eating disorder is compulsive overeating, which can lead to obesity or make someone who's slightly overweight become morbidly overweight.

Eating disorders usually develop during the teenage years, but they're showing up more frequently in girls as young as 7. In a recent survey of fifth- to eighth-grade girls, 9 percent said they occasionally fasted and 5 percent had forced themselves to vomit to lose weight. Thirty-one percent of these girls said that they were on a diet, an ominous finding itself since, along with being female, being on a diet is one of the biggest risk factors for developing an eating disorder.

Not every girl who diets ends up with an eating disorder, of course, and experts have had a hard time pinning down just what makes a girl go over the edge. Some have blamed Barbie, with her unrealistically slim waist. Mattel has responded by reshaping the most popular toy of all times with a somewhat wider waist and hip girth. But eating disorders continue to increase. Researchers have also cited the fashion magazines, with their almost anorexic-looking models, as a cause of anorexia and bulimia, since young girls who read these magazines see beauty equated with extreme thinness. But it now seems that "the Media" have about as much to do with eating disorders as they do with youth violence. Skinny beauty queens and gory films and video games may contribute to these problems, respectively, but they don't cause them.

New research suggests that a constellation of experiences that affect mainly girls promote eating disorders. Perhaps the first such experience is for a girl to watch and hear her mother regularly fret about being fat and talk about going on a diet so she can look good in a bathing suit. A young girl may learn from Mom's example that dieting is something that females have to do to be attractive. At school, more girls than boys are teased about their weight. A heavy boy may be admired as a powerful slugger on the baseball team, but a heavy girl stands a greater chance of being ostracized and called "fat" or "ugly." So, it's easy to see why a girl may come to think that if she could only be thinner, she'd be prettier and more popular.

Add to pretty and popular the goal of being a good athlete or dancer. Being lightweight and slim is an advantage in certain activities that attract a lot of girls, like running, gymnastics, and ballet. So anorexia and bulimia are especially common among female athletes. Researchers estimate that as many as 62 percent of girls and women in sports have disordered eating habits, compared with about 3 percent to 6 percent of females overall. (For more information, see Female Athlete Triad, pages 245–46.)

Clearly, girls grow up with powerful experiences that focus their attention on their body shape and size, but an overarching desire to be thin isn't the only cause of eating disorders or even the main cause. Being a perfectionist is the biggest predictor of who will develop an eating disorder, bigger than being female, said Marcia Herrin, codirector of the Eating Disorders Prevention, Education and Treatment Program at Dartmouth College. "People with eating disorders say losing weight isn't what it's about for them," Herrin pointed out. "It's more complicated. For them, it's about being perfect and being in control." Somehow, excelling in whatever activities they're into, whether they are certain sports or fine arts or academic subjects at school, becomes wrapped up with imposing control over their body shape and size.

When Herrin explains the connection between personality and eating disorders to the parents of the students she treats, the parents often look back and realize that the signs of perfectionism were there all along. "Parents will say, 'Of course! She was obsessed with doing perfect schoolwork,'" she said.

Whether it's possible to prevent eating disorders by helping a girl to temper her extreme perfectionism is unknown. Herrin does suggest other preventive measures, such as talking to your daughters early on about the dangers of eating disorders.

Given that perfectionism carries the risk of eating disorders, a natural question for parents is how can they support their daughters' high standards at school, in sports, and in other activities without the unhealthy consequences? There's no easy answer, but Herrin thinks that one constructive step that parents can take is to look for signs that their children are stressed out from too many after-school activities. In Herrin's view, overscheduling tends to go along with parents' high expectations for their children. For some children, she thinks that all the pressure of going from violin lessons to ballet to softball practice is too much to bear. And one of the ways girls crumble under the pressure is to develop abnormal eating habits. "Parents are part of the reason why kids aim toward perfectionism," Herrin said. "Many parents imagine a fast track for their children, but they need to consider the it's-good-enough approach." If more girls kicked back and had a little more time to themselves, she thinks fewer of them would have eating disorders.

That may be so, but not all hard-driving, overscheduled perfectionists develop eating disorders. Research suggests that some girls have a biological predisposition to them. It seems likely that a high-pressured lifestyle may trigger eating disorders in girls who are predisposed. Recent research suggests that bulimia is due, at least in part, to abnormally low levels of serotonin, the hormone that's also associated with depression and some other psychiatric disorders. Low levels of serotonin may be involved with anorexia as well, Herrin said, since Prozac, an antidepressant that enhances serotonin, is used successfully to treat patients with bulimia and anorexia. One reason why eating disorders are especially common in teenage girls is that these girls' serotonin levels are in a state of flux—they rise and fall with the levels of estrogen and progesterone, which are fairly unstable during adolescence.

PAIN

The DTP—diphtheria, tetanus, and pertussus—shot is one of the most painful routine childhood immunizations. And the worst DTP is the booster shot that's scheduled between ages 4 and 6 because it's the one that children get when they're old enough to anticipate and fear the pain. Nurses and pediatricians recommend that parents prepare their children ahead of time and reassure them that even though the shot will hurt, it will protect them from illnesses that hurt more. To sweeten the deal, the experts suggest promising children a reward afterward.

I followed this advice with my son and my daughter, in each case with different effects. David howled in agony, shouting that the shot was the "baddest thing in the whole world" as he lay sobbing in my arms. Sarah didn't flinch as she sat on the examining table. Are my children typical of boys and girls in general—do girls tolerate pain better than boys? The idea that they do fits a common stereotype about males: that despite their tough-guy exterior, they can't handle pain. "Imagine," mothers love to say, "if *men* had to go through childbirth . . . "

But my experience illustrates how hard it is to draw sweeping conclusions based on your own children. As it turns out, my children are atypical. Researchers have just begun to look at differences in boys' and girls' perceptions of pain. In studies that compare children's reactions (such as crying) to painful experiences like injuries and medical procedures and their ratings of the pain's intensity, girls, for the most part, show and describe more pain than do boys. The same is true for women and men.

One reason why girls admit to feeling more pain is that society allows them greater freedom to do so. They're under less pressure to act tough, and they talk more about how they feel. Girls' greater expressiveness is a factor, but even when it's taken into account, girls still feel more kinds of pain more intensely than do boys. That was the conclusion of a conference on gender and pain held by NIH in 1998.

Girls get more headaches and stomachaches. They're more bothered by immunizations, intravenous punctures, and broken bones. Far more girls than boys complain of pain that has no known physical cause, like fibromyalgia, which is widespread pain and extreme tenderness, and reflex sympathetic dystrophy, a pain syndrome with burning, coldness, and other strange sensations in the arms and legs. Oddly enough, for some reason the only kind of pain that boys report feeling more intensely is the pain from orthodontists tightening their braces.

It's too early to say what causes sex differences in the perception of pain, but sex hormones almost certainly are involved. Women are most sensitive to certain kinds of pain in the two weeks before their periods, when estrogen and progesterone plunge from their monthly high. And throughout the month, women with the highest overall levels of estradiol, a form of estrogen, are more sensitive to pain than are other women. There's some evidence from studies of rats that estrogen heightens sensitivity to pain and testosterone lowers it.

Extreme sensitivity to pain is also tied up with emotional problems, like anxiety and depression. In fact, hypochondria—the experience of pain and other symptoms with no physical cause—is a sign of depression. Although hypochondria appears to affect equal numbers of boys and girls before adolescence, it's more common in girls during adolescence, when their depression rates are soaring. Doctors at Harvard who are studying girls with reflex sympathetic dystrophy, a pain syndrome that affects 6 girls to every boy, have noticed that many of these girls also suffer from anxiety, depression, and eating disorders.

Since boys and girls feel pain differently, it's only natural to wonder if it should be treated differently. Researchers have found that ibuprofen, the popular pain reliever, is less effective in women than in men, but the same isn't true for all painkillers. Women who have had impacted molars pulled get better pain relief than do men from two different opioid analgesics— pentazocine and nalbuphine. It's not known whether certain painkillers are more effective in boys and others in girls.

For the time being, a more pressing issue for parents than whether their children should get ibuprofen or acetaminophen is how to make sure that doctors and nurses take their children's pain seriously. Many of the most physically painful experiences of childhood occur in hospitals and doctors' offices, noted Patricia McGrath, director of the Paediatric Pain Program at the University of Western Ontario in Canada, yet all too often children's pain is undertreated or untreated. Drugs aren't always needed to relieve children's pain. McGrath has found that giving a child as much control as possible over a medical procedure can significantly decrease his or her pain. Doing so can mean asking a 5 year old to decide which arm she gets her DPT booster shot in or giving a 7 year old with leukemia the freedom not only to pick which finger will be pricked for a routine blood test but to do the finger prick herself.

PERVASIVE DEVELOPMENTAL DISORDERS

From the time James was a baby, he showed no pleasure in other people's company. He didn't like to be cuddled. He didn't gesture to be picked up. The older he got, the more antisocial he became. As a toddler and a preschooler, when other children his age were pretending to feed dolls or drive cars, James didn't pretend to do any of the things that people do. He didn't want to play with anybody. "He was more interested in objects than in people," recalls his father, a pediatrician in the Midwest.

James has autism, a brain disorder that, above all else, robs people of their social sense and sensibility. It also clouds rational thinking and disables the imagination. Autism is one of a spectrum of five similar conditions that fall under the umbrella of pervasive developmental disorder. Each of the conditions shows a strong gender difference. Autism is four times as common in boys as in girls. Three of the related developmental disorders affect more boys, too. The fifth and most devastating of the disorders, Rett syndrome, occurs only in girls and was recently traced to a faulty gene.

The cause of the other pervasive developmental disorders is unknown, but the male-versus-female pattern, coupled with the tendency of the disorders to run in families, indicates that they, too, are at least partially genetic. Scientists think that some of the genes involved may control brain development and that defects in these genes interfere with it. Brain-imaging studies of people with pervasive developmental disorders reveal abnormalities in several areas of the brain that control social intelligence: certain medial temporal lobe structures, the amygdala, the hippocampus, and the cerebellum. Even though the symptoms of pervasive developmental disorders usually don't show up until a child is about $1\frac{1}{2}$ years old, scientists think that the underlying brain problems arise long before birth when the brain is forming.

Why the gender differences? A leading theory is that the genetic defects that cause pervasive developmental disorders are linked to sex chromosomes. That's the case with the Rett gene, which lies on the X chromosome. Girls have two X chromosomes, which means that they have two copies of the Rett gene; boys have just one. Scientists think that Rett syndrome occurs when girls inherit one damaged copy of the gene and one normal copy. The likely reason why boys don't get Rett syndrome is that inheriting a defective Rett gene without a normal copy to compensate for it is fatal.

It's possible that autism is also caused by a gene on the X chromosome, as is the case with Fragile X, a form of mental retardation that affects only males. In this case, the one and only copy of the defective gene wouldn't be fatal; it would trigger autism. In girls, inheriting one normal copy of the gene may protect them from the disorder, as happens with Fragile X. But having the gene would make them carriers of the condition, which they could then can pass on to their sons.

Genes aren't completely to blame. Under certain conditions, viruses may trigger autism. Several decades ago, doctors discovered that women who had German measles during the first trimester of pregnancy gave birth to more autistic children than was average. Doctors think that pieces of the rubella virus migrated into the fetuses' brains and prevented the formation of certain circuitry. Boys may be at a higher risk of such interference since their brains develop more slowly than girls', leaving them more vulnerable to damage.

There's yet another curious boy-girl difference with pervasive developmental disorders. Although boys have the highest risk, girls tend to have the most severe cases—more of them are mentally retarded in addition to being socially disabled. Doctors think that the difference may relate to girls' strength in reading social cues. If girls are born with a greater capacity for social understanding—and there's evidence that they are (see Chapter 2, pages 54–58)—a mild problem with socialization may go unnoticed. It may take a severe form of illness to rob a girl of her social acumen to such a degree that she appears ill. "This is quite speculative," said Dr. Edwin Cook, a psychologist at the University of Chicago who's been studying the genetics of autism, "but it may simply be that a decreased risk of the social component means that you have to be more mentally retarded to be seen as having autism."

What the sex difference in autism means for parents is that it may take more frequent and intensive therapy, more time, and more patience to help their daughters improve compared with their sons. Children with milder forms of pervasive developmental disorder—social impairment but normal intelligence—have the best chance of responding to mainstays of treatment, like behavior therapy and language therapy, which aim to develop their sense of social give-and-take. Children with severe illness may need therapy just to get them to the point that they can begin to learn social skills.

SPORTS INJURIES

When Shelli was 12, she developed a symptom that she associated more with her grandparents' generation than with her own. Her left knee would lock up and become so stiff that she had trouble bending it. Shelli's doctor recommended physical therapy, and the problem went away for a while. But it returned with a vengeance about a year later, shortly after she started playing on the volleyball team at her middle school in New York City. As the volleyball season progressed, so did the stiffness and pain in her knee.

Shelli soon realized that far from being a sign of old age, knee problems were fairly common among the girls who played sports at her school. Much of the talk in the locker room was about orthopedic surgeons, MRIs, and knee surgery. It turned out that Shelli had a torn meniscus, cartilage in the knee. Several players on the girls' volleyball team and the girls' softball team had tears of the anterior cruciate, one of four major ligaments that helps hold the knee joint in place. Shelli and some of the other girls had surgery, followed by many weeks of physical therapy, before they could return to the field and court.

Now that a significant number of girls are playing sports, they're getting more of the muscle pulls, torn ligaments, and other sports injuries that have long plagued boys. But doctors who mend sports injuries have noticed a curious trend. Even when boys and girls play the same sports, girls have a somewhat higher injury rate. Doctors see the difference in children under age 12, but it becomes more common and pronounced in the teenage years as the level of play grows more demanding.

Girls' higher risk of sports injuries shouldn't be taken as proof of the outmoded view that girls are too weak or delicate to play sports. Quite to the contrary, the benefits of athletics outweigh the risks. Girls who participate in sports or exercise regularly have lower rates of obesity and depression and do better in school than unathletic girls. Girls can play as hard as the boys. Their injury rate isn't a sign of weakness. Instead, it's a sign that girls' training needs are different from boys'—that was the conclusion of a workshop on health and female athletes held in 1999 by the American Academy of Orthopedic Surgeons and NIH.

It's no coincidence that Shelli and many of her classmates

damaged their knees. The knees are where the gender difference in sports injuries is the greatest, although stress fractures and injuries to shoulders, elbows, and ankles are also more common in female athletes. Knee injuries are about four times as common in girls as in boys. The risk is greatest in basketball, soccer, volleyball, and softball, sports with a lot of high-impact moves like hard jumps, pivots, and sudden turns, all of which place a lot of stress on the knees. The most common knee injury is a tear of the anterior cruciate, or ACL.

Sports doctors are only beginning to look at why girls are more prone to certain injuries, but they've focused most of their attention on the knees because they've had to repair so many of them lately. Girls' knees are more vulnerable for several reasons, some having to do with nature, others with nurture. One important factor is muscle strength. Although boys and girls are almost equally strong before puberty, boys become stronger in adolescence. Boys' muscles are stronger throughout the body, but this strength is especially important in the knees because so much of the force of running, jumping, twisting, turning, and other athletic movements travels right to them, pulling their muscles and ligaments every which way and sending shock waves through the cartilage.

The stronger the knee muscles, the more stable the knee is when buffeted about. The most critical muscles for stabilizing the knee are the hamstrings, which run behind the knee and enable it to bend. Ideally, the hamstrings should be 60 percent to 70 percent as strong as the quadriceps, the muscles that straighten the knee, but girls' hamstrings are just 49 percent to 55 percent as strong as their quadriceps. When the hamstrings aren't strong enough to stabilize the knee, the ligaments and quadriceps have to do more work and get more wear and tear.

Other anatomical features seem to take a toll on girls' knees.

For one thing, the ACL itself is smaller in relation to overall body weight in females than in males, so it tears more easily. And the ACL and other ligaments and tendons are looser in females than in males. Female athletes' posture also increases the risk of knee injuries. Girls and women run and land from a jump in a more upright position than do boys and men. This position puts more force on their quadriceps. The quadriceps can then pull the shinbone too far forward, an action that can tear the ACL.

So much for the nature component. Here's now nurture works against girls' knees. Although teenage boys are naturally stronger than teenage girls, they also have more opportunity to strengthen their muscles through training. Even when they're playing the same sports, boys get better training, researchers say. This gender bias was obvious to Shelli. "In preseason volleyball training, we ran a lot and stretched, but the guys' teams were doing weight training," she said. Research shows that girls' knee-injury rate can be reduced by training programs geared specifically to girls: strengthening the hamstrings and other muscles and learning to run and jump in a more crouched position.

There's less certainty about how to prevent other sports-related health problems that are common to girls. Girls are more prone to stress fractures than boys. Doctors don't completely understand why, but one factor is a triad of disorders that's common to some excessively hard-driving female athletes: osteoporosis, a poor diet, and irregular periods. Girls and women with the female athlete triad feel so compelled to be thin for peak performance that they don't eat enough. Their eating pattern may not be extreme enough to be considered an eating disorder, but they're still undernourished. Without enough body fat, their estrogen level falls too low to maintain proper bone mass and a regular menstrual cycle. So they develop osteoporosis, a thinning of the bones that puts them at risk of fractures.

There's been considerable publicity about eating disorders in professional athletes, like Christy Henrich, a world-class gymnast who died at age 22. But the female athlete triad isn't a problem only of elite professional athletes; it affects girls, too, especially those who participate in sports that emphasize low body weight, like gymnastics, figure skating, swimming, and distance running. So, if your daughter is athletic, talk to her about the risks of the triad. It's really up to you to take the lead in prevention, since coaches don't routinely talk about it and doctors don't usually notice the symptoms during annual physical exams. If your daughter comes back with the argument that she's got to lose weight to do well, tell her that losing too much weight can weaken her performance and threaten her life.

SUMMING UP

Research on gender differences in physical and emotional health is in its infancy, but already it's clear that males and females do not face the same risks for a wide range of health problems, including accidental injuries, sports injuries, asthma, anxiety, depression, and eating disorders. Even when they do have the same illnesses, they don't always have the same symptoms or even the same responses to certain medications. These differences are due to biological factors in some cases, such as gender differences in the immune system and the brain. But social factors like gender bias also play a role, and they can be modified to protect girls from certain health problems and boys from others.

Not enough is known for doctors to prescribe different treatments for boys and girls when they have the same ailments, but that may change. Research on gender differences in health is gaining momentum and respect within the medical community. Less than a decade ago, new drugs were tested mainly on men, and their effects were extrapolated to women. Now, NIH requires that women be included in new drug trials to account for possible gender differences in the drugs' safety and effectiveness. In 1998, Congress went even further and directed the Department of Health and Human Services to finance a report that would outline the questions about gender and health that researchers should study. Once there are answers, checking the male or female box on a medical form may turn out be more than just a formality; it could signal how best to prevent, diagnose, and treat ailments in our children and ourselves.

SUGGESTIONS FOR PARENTS

Just being aware of the health problems with gender differences can benefit your child by helping you recognize and treat the problems early. But doctors in the vanguard of gender-based medicine have found that parents can help prevent several of these problems by acting to change the situations that put their sons and daughters at risk. Preventable problems include accidental injuries in boys; depression in girls and boys; and adult-onset diabetes, eating disorders, and sports-related health problems in girls.

Talk, Don't Preach, About Risky Behavior.   Boys wind up in the emergency room with more broken arms, burns, and other accidental injuries than girls because they're more willing to take common childhood risks, like riding a bike without a helmet; jumping off the top of a slide; or, even as toddlers, grabbing a hot coffee cup. Lecturing risk takers on what they should and shouldn't do is ineffective, said Barbara Morrongiello, who does research on sex difference in risk taking. One reason why boys take more risks than girls is that they don't believe that they'll get hurt. But Morrongiello has found that explaining the painful or dangerous consequences of specific risks can help boys size them up more realistically and think before they act.

Don't Ruminate.   Mothers and daughters are good at talking about how they feel—especially when they're feeling blue. But the habit of ruminating on negative events or sadness is one of the key factors that makes girls vulnerable to depression, said Susan Nolen-Hoeksema. Depression is twice as common in teenage girls as in teenage boys, and even before the teen years, girls are more given to rumination than boys, Nolen-Hoeksema said. She thinks that mothers can help prevent depression in their daughters by discouraging rumination. This doesn't mean cutting your daughter off when she wants to pour her heart out. Nolen-Hoeksema said that it's important to acknowledge the hurt, but that it's equally important to help your daughter come up with ways to deal with it.

Here's an example. Let's say your 10-year-old daughter comes home crying because a classmate told her she was ugly. First, talk about how painful the experience was, then ask your daughter why that particular person told her she was ugly and if she herself believes that this is true. The conversation can then progress to ways that your daughter can stand up to this class-mate. "You want to help her avoid wallowing in her sadness or withdrawing from the person," Nolen-Hoeksema said. "One example is to say, 'I don't know why you need to tell me that I'm ugly, but it really makes me feel rotten when you do.' A lot of kids back off when they hear something like this."

Help Your Son Lead a Double Life.   By the time they're in elementary school, many boys refuse to hug or kiss their parents good-bye anywhere near their classmates for fear of being branded sissies by the guys. The self-imposed ban on public displays of affection is a symptom of a larger problem—that many boys have trouble showing emotion because they think they've got to act tough. So, they deny or play down their feelings, especially when something bad happens. But psychologists think that holding in their feelings can contribute to depression, which is more common in young boys than it is in young girls. It may also put them at risk of substance abuse and violence.

The situation creates a dilemma for parents: How can you help your sons open up when you know as well as they do that if they wear their hearts on their sleeves, the other guys may laugh? Peggy McIntosh, codirector of the National SEED Project on educational equity and diversity, thinks that it's time that we teach our sons a survival strategy that girls and women have used for years: Lead a double life.

As girls' lives have grown more competitive, with their increased participation in sports and higher education and career goals, they've had to learn how to be tough when the situation demands it. But they also know that they can let down their guard in private. They understand that being soft doesn't take away from their toughness, and vice versa. McIntosh thinks that parents can help boys understand this concept by giving them safe and private opportunities to show their soft side.

Carol Nagy Jacklin helped her son get comfortable with the double-life concept several years ago, when he was in elementary school. Her son didn't want to kiss her good-bye at school, but he wanted to kiss her good-bye. So when she drove him to school each morning, she'd stop the car two blocks away for a hug and kiss in private. Then they'd continue on to school, and he'd get out of the car with a nonchalant wave.

Keep Your Son Talking. That's easier said than done, as any parent knows who has asked, "So, what did you do in school today" and had his or her son shrug or walk right by without answering. But the difficulty that boys have opening up may increase their risk of depression. How, exactly, do you get your son to talk? Here are some parent-tested techniques.

Go for a drive. Boys are more comfortable talking if they don't think they're "supposed" to talk. They're more apt to open up if you're not looking directly at them. Faye Chaplin, codirector of the Community Nursery School in Dobbs Ferry, New York, said that she's had some of the best conversations with her sons while she was keeping her eyes on the road.

Share some activity. Driving isn't the only way to loosen up your son for conversation. Play a computer game or card game or play catch. Get interested in what interests him. Any shared activity will keep you connected with your son, giving him the opportunity to talk when he's ready.

When he wants to talk, drop everything. Like a cat that won't come when called but will throw himself at your feet purring when he's in the mood, boys like to make the first move when it comes to talking. My son tends to want to talk at just the times when I don't—like after I've kissed him goodnight. But we've had some of our most important conversations after I turned the lights off in his room: How he felt when a friend stopped being his friend, how people get over the death of a loved one, what HIV stands for, and how you get it.

Build Your Child's Social Skills. Coaching children in the tricky business of interpersonal relations can help prevent depression in girls as well as boys. Martin Seligman and his colleagues at the University of Pennsylvania developed a group therapy program for 10- to 13-year-old boys and girls who were at risk of clinical depression. In the after-school sessions, the children learned to recognize and change negative ways of thinking, be assertive with peers, and use peaceful means of settling conflicts. The program had a lasting impact. Seligman followed one group of children for two years after they'd finished the sessions. He found that the incidence of depression was half that of a control group of children.

Start Early to Prevent Eating Disorders. Eating disorders are becoming so common among girls that experts suggest that parents educate their daughters about the risks of eating disorders much as they do about drugs, smoking, and alcohol. Marcia Herrin, an expert in eating disorders, started her educational campaign with her daughter when she was still in preschool. Here are the preventive measures that Herrin recommends:

Don't talk about dieting. If you're on a diet, keep it to yourself. Girls whose mothers complain about their own "weight problem" are more likely than other girls to worry about their weight and eventually start dieting. Dieting is dangerous for children because it can deprive them of calories needed for growth. And going on a diet is one of the biggest risk factors for developing an eating disorder.

Give a brief genetics lesson. Simply tell your child that a person's normal body weight and size are 70 percent genetic, Herrin said, which means that, for the most part, they're beyond control. This isn't to say that you and your child should pay no attention to her weight. Tell her that eating healthy foods (lots of fruits and vegetables and few high-fat and sugary snacks) and having regular physical activity can help keep her weight normal, which is to say neither overweight nor underweight for her.

Say why "too thin" is as unhealthy as "too fat." Your child may understand all too clearly the downsides of being overweight, but she may not realize that being underweight is bad, too. Tell her that eating too little deprives the body of enough fuel. In addition to interfering with normal growth, inadequate food intake can make a person sick, causing brittle bones; general weakness; and, in extreme cases, death.

Show that beauty comes in all shapes and sizes. Point out celebrities and other people of different sizes who are good-looking to let your child know that there's no single standard of beauty. "With my 11-year-old daughter, we talk about popular singers who are heavy and attractive," Herrin said.

Know the warning signs of eating disorders. People with eating disorders are good at hiding them. Your child may eat a normal amount of food in front of you, but not eat when she's away from you, at school or with friends. Or, she may secretly force herself to vomit to lose weight. Still, there are some warning signs. Most obviously, does your daughter look thinner or much heavier? Does she make remarks that indicate that she's unhappy with her weight? Has your daughter's period stopped for three months straight? If she's 16, has she never had a period? If you suspect that your daughter's eating habits aren't normal, schedule an appointment with a doctor who has experience treating eating disorders.

Don't dwell on your daughter's appearance. One mother confessed that she never told her daughter that she looked beautiful for fear of making her value her looks more than her abilities. She didn't realize that her view was over the top until she saw the horrified reaction of a friend, who is a mother and a psychiatrist, who said that she felt that praise of all kinds was good for all children.

The question is, How do you strike a balance? Research does show that vanity can cause girls to have strong feelings of shame about their bodies, which can then lead to anxiety, depression, and eating disorders. Among the main things that girls ruminate about is their appearance, and rumination contributes to depression. Still, don't be afraid to tell your daughter when she looks nice. But praise her more for her effort, grace, coordination, and other accomplishments than for her appearance.

Encourage Your Daughter to Be Physically Active. Playing on a sports team, dancing, or exercising regularly can help prevent two health problems that are more common in girls: depression and adult-onset diabetes. Being active is a powerful hedge against depression for girls because it helps shift their attention away from how they look to what they can do. And regular, vigorous physical activity can lower a girl's risk of adult-onset diabetes by helping to prevent obesity, a leading cause of the illness. Doctors think the reason why the incidence of this type of diabetes is climbing in girls is that girls are less active and more obese than boys.

Monitor Your Daughter's Sports Training. Girls get more injuries, especially knee injuries, than boys when they play the same sports. An important reason is that their muscles are weaker because they get less training. Sports doctors have found that when girls get special training to strengthen their muscles and when they're taught to run and land from a jump in a more crouched position, their rate of knee injuries goes down. Such training is especially important for basketball, softball, volleyball, and soccer. If your daughter's coach isn't aware of the latest research, bring him or her up to date.

Dave Oliver, the strength and conditioning coach for the United States Women's Soccer team, starts with girls by age 8, having them build muscle strength with pushups and other resistance exercises. Beginning at age 12, he recommends that girls do weight training.

Sports doctors at the Cincinnati Sportsmedicine Research and Education Institute designed a six-week preseason training program for high school girls who play soccer, basketball, volleyball, and other sports. It's similar to the women's soccer training except that it also teaches the girls to jump more safely, with their knees bent and less side-to-side or forward-backward motion. The Cincinnati doctors have found that their program reduces the rate of knee injuries in female high school athletes fourfold to fivefold.

Beware of the Female Athlete Triad.   Training too hard can put your daughter at risk of the female athletic triad: eating disorders, amenorrhea (irregular or missing periods), and osteoporosis. The problem begins when a girl works out so intensely that she loses a lot of weight or goes on a diet because she thinks that losing weight will improve her performance. Either way, the weight loss lowers her estrogen level to the point that she can't menstruate regularly and may develop osteoporosis, thinning of the bones, which increases the risk of fractures and other injuries.

The American College of Sports Medicine recommends that girls and women with just one component of the female athlete triad see a doctor and be screened for the other two. So, if your daughter is athletic, keep an eye on her eating habits and her weight and ask her about her periods. If she's missed three periods in a row, she may not be eating well enough, so her doctor should check her for symptoms of disordered eating, such as weight loss or depression, and symptoms of bone loss, such as stress fractures. If she has any of these symptoms, she should see a doctor with experience treating eating disorders. The first step in treating the female athlete triad is to get the child eating a healthy diet, then to arrange for counseling for low self-esteem, depression, and other psychological factors that may have led to her disordered eating in the first place.

Afterword

Nature versus Nurture

The wealth of recent gender research has helped answer many of parents' most frequently asked questions about what makes boys and girls tick. It has identified key differences in their brains, as well as in the ways that parents, teachers, and other people treat boys and girls. It has shown how nature—a child's biology—commingles with nurture—a child's upbringing and experiences—to yield gender differences in behavior, personality, interests, school performance, and health. It has exploded some long-standing myths about girls and boys.

And your sons and daughters stand to benefit from the research. This book has shown how you can use it to help your children avoid gender biases that can inhibit their social and intellectual development and harm their health and well-being. But how much of an effect do individual parents really have? How can you be sure that *your* child will grow to overcome the confines of gender stereotypes?

It's hard to have faith that everything will work out in the end when the news is filled with reports of social ills linked to gender-typed behavior and attitudes: Violence committed by young boys, sexual harassment at school, eating disorders among girls who are desperate to be pretty and perfect. These are complex problems, and it's naive to think that parents alone can enough to solve them. Social biases push males and females in different and often destructive directions, and so does biology. But which force pushes harder and has a more enduring influence?

About a century ago, when the scientific study of gender differences began in earnest, researchers attempted to prove that females were less intelligent, weaker, and generally less capable than males because of basic biological differences. Then, during the feminist movement, researchers swept aside biological differences as being unimportant. Instead, they showed how social biases held girls and women back. Now, that it's possible to see gender differences in the working brain and in the genes and to measure them in hormone levels and in the immune system, biological differences are grabbing the spotlight once again. The question is, are they grabbing too much of it and making us believe that there's little we can do to change nature?

When scientists uncover gender differences in the brain or in genes, we pay attention. Biological differences are sexy. But beware. They're often misinterpreted and given more importance than they deserve. Specific, highly technical or even tentative findings have been mistakenly held up as proof that males and females have different levels of ability.

For example, several years ago, Yale researchers reported that women use both sides of their brains when reading, whereas men use just the right side. This was a landmark study that made headlines. But laypeople and some scientists alike jumped to the conclusion that females give over more of their brains to *all* language tasks and that this explains why girls have an easier time learning to read and write. Some educators even thought the research proved that boys were basically inferior readers and writers and justified holding them to lower standards than girls in these areas. Biology was destiny, after all.

On follow-up, however, the Yale researchers found that females' brains were less lateralized only for specific reading tasks, namely, linking sounds with words, not for most other aspects of reading, like comprehension and building vocabulary. There is no evidence that the female pattern is better for practical matters like learning to read and crafting a sentence. So even though the male and female brains read differently in one respect, they're not necessarily unequal in reading ability.

Over the years, other biological differences have been cited as proof of gender differences in ability. For a while, differences in brain structure and hormone levels were held up as evidence that girls were hopelessly inferior in math and certain spatial skills. Testosterone, the thinking went, somehow wired the brain for excellence in these areas. But again biological findings proved not to be destiny. The gender gap in math has nearly closed as a result of a combination of efforts to eliminate gender biases in school and to require all students to take more math classes. And it is now clear that spatial skills improve with practice.

Consider another biological difference, one long used as an excuse to keep females out of sports: Men are stronger than women. No one could dispute that fact. But females' comparatively weaker muscles were once considered a reason (along with their "delicate" reproductive organs) why girls and women don't have what it takes to play "male" sports like basketball and soccer professionally or on a world-class level. Wrong again. The Women's National Basketball Association and the United States women's soccer team make a mockery of that theory.

Despite gender differences in biology, females have been entering traditionally male fields like professional sports, law, and medicine for years. More recently, males have started to tread on traditionally female territory, working as au pairs and baby-sitters, debunking notions about males' lack of a nurturing instinct. Parents who wouldn't have considered hiring a male nanny a few years ago are hiring them now. Our children are growing up with more options and less gender bias than we did. And we have the power to push the trend even further.

Just how much influence biology has on a child's potential has yet to be learned. But we do know that when parents and other important adults think a child is inferior at things like math, sports, and language arts, the child, regardless of his or her demonstrated ability, comes to think so, too. And children who don't believe in themselves don't try to do as well as they can. Biological differences may endow boys and girls with different strengths and weaknesses to start with, but experience shows that they don't close doors. The support of parents, the inspiration of teachers and coaches, and equal opportunity can offset biological differences to bring out the best in each child.